I0129116

Rosina Lytton

Shells from the Sands of Time

Rosina Lytton

Shells from the Sands of Time

ISBN/EAN: 9783743308565

Manufactured in Europe, USA, Canada, Australia, Japa

Cover: Foto ©Thomas Meinert / pixelio.de

Manufactured and distributed by brebook publishing software
(www.brebook.com)

Rosina Lytton

Shells from the Sands of Time

SHELLS from the SANDS of TIME

SHELLS FROM THE SANDS

OF TIME.

SHELLS FROM THE SANDS

OF TIME.

BY

THE DOWAGER LADY LYTTON.

LONDON:

BICKERS AND SON, I, LEICESTER SQUARE.

1876.

CHISWICK PRESS:—PRINTED BY WHITTINGHAM AND WILKINS,
TOOKS COURT, CHANCERY LANE.

CONTENTS.

ON BAD MANNERS.

OUR friend, the German poet, historian, metaphysician, and portrait painter, quoted by Burton, but whose name, unfortunately (not to say unfairly), has not descended to posterity, by his revelations about England, reminds us of the debt of gratitude we still continue to incur to "distinguished foreigners," for eternally pointing out to us mines of vice and mountains of virtue which, without their kind intervention, our own indigenous perceptions would neither have been sufficiently elevated nor profound to have discovered; and even when they note a palpable and indisputable fact, they generally prop it up with an auxiliary or mine it with a motive that we natives ignored before. Thus, the French *will* have it to this day, that English women are insanely *romantic*, it has even passed into a proverb with them—*romanesque comme une*

Anglaife :" and as they are the only people who
go to war for an idea, fo are they the only people who generoufly and gratuitoufly graft their
ideas on the numfkulls of other nations, and in
fo doing, they have decided that this "given"
romantic mania of Englifh women has its origin
in tea, toaft, green veils, and grooms ; that is,
from an over-indulgence in the three former,
and from young ladies (*des jeunes* "*meeffes*")
being allowed to ride out *fola* with the latter.
This was the ftereotyped French theory of the
eighteenth century, and neither the intercourfe
of a fixty or forty years' peace, nor a confequently nearer view of, and more intimate
acquaintance with, bottled porter, beef-fteaks,
and Balmoral boots, has at all been able to
difpel this "romantic" idea from French
brains. The next chimera, not only of the
French, but of moft continental peoples, is
the exceeding domefticity and love of home
of the *male* as well as the female fpecimen of the
Anglo-Saxon. They have an *idée fixe* that even *mi
Lord Bull*, in the higheft claffes, is benevolently
addicted to balancing his own babies, while my
Lady Bull is equally perfevering in fewing on
fhirt buttons, and offering her mafter the de-
ferential homage of a filent admiration,—in fhort,
that an Englifhman, like a fnail, can with difficulty be got to protrude his head beyond his

houfe, as is clearly demonftrated by our Clubs, ceafelefs continental tours, and univerfal *domophobia* in the upper claffes ; and the gin-palace, the tap-room, and the " ring," in the lower. But Henrich Heine, in his " RIEISBILDER," is kind enough to point out the *caufe* of this exceeding ftay-at-homeativenefs among Englifhmen ; and here it is, in all its ftartling novelty and profundity :—" L'Anglais cherche cette fatiffaction de l'âme (dans fon intérieur) que fa gaucherie naturelle, fous le rapport focial, lui interdit hors de chez-lui."[1]

It is certain that good manners are our national deficiency, and bad ones, our national curfe. This is fo patent, that marvels are made of the few exceptions that prove the rule, and we conftantly hear, as a noticeable and memorable thing, after a brief *réfumé* of a perfon's focial virtues or fhortcomings, as the cafe may be,—" But then Lady ——, Lord ——, Mr. This, or Mrs. That, have fuch charming manners," as in other countries perfons are cited for their fcientific or artiftic attainments. Nor does this *gaucherie*, fhynefs,

---

[1] " An Englifhman feeks that internal felf-complacency at his own firefide which his natural awkwardnefs of manner in regard to all focial intercourfe precludes his enjoying beyond his own family circle." Granted the awkwardnefs of manner, but denied that it takes refuge in, and confines itfelf to, its own chimney-corner. Would that it did !

or whatever you choofe to call it, fo much origi-
nate in pride, as in felfifhnefs. An Englifhman's
firft dread, in extending a civility, or venturing
upon anything like acquaintancefhip with
ftrangers, is, that it *may* by fome remote
poffibility entail boredom upon him of fome
fort; and from his earlieft dawn the Anglo-
Saxon has been in the habit of referring everything to felf, and never troubling his head what
effect that very difagreeable autocrat may produce upon others; hence, the ill breeding and,
in many inftances, pofitive bearifhnefs of brothers and fons to their mothers and fifters, and
of hufbands to their wives and daughters. And
what we have not in our own homes, depend upon it, we cannot take out into the world with
us; and though a more gracious and courteous
bearing may now and then be borrowed, like
plate or jewels, for fome fpecial occafion, they
are not *ours*, and form no part of us. The root
of good breeding is Chriftianity; and the effence
of genuine Chriftianity is *gratuitous and difin-
terefted kindnefs.* If among all our job com-
miffionerfhips we only had commiffioners of
good breeding, and its evidence, good manners,
the only teft they could poffibly obtain for the
difcovery of real gentlemen and gentlewomen
would be to fee them (unknown to the faid
gentlemen and gentlewomen) with their inferiors,

or with thofe who were under obligations to them, or who wanted their fervices. For as the devil can quote Scripture to further his own ends, fo even the moft felfifh and ill-bred perfons can be the moft amiable, *empreffé*, and *prévenant*, if they have a point to carry ; but the point once carried, the boundary wall once fcaled, fuch perfons are apt to kick down the ladder too foon, never recollecting that it might again be *wanted* at fome future time ; for it is part of the fubtle chemiftry of God's retributive juftice that nothing fhould be fo narrow and fhort-fighted as Selfifhnefs,—that ftrange, many-handed, no-hearted monfter, which is at once the parent and the offspring of every vice.

In a quaint old book, tranflated into Englifh in 1730, and written by one DON BALTASAR GRATIAN, the Locke of Spain, entitled " The Compleat Gentleman, or a Defcription of the feveral Qualifications, both Natural and Acquired, that are neceffary to form a Great Man," and dedicated by the tranflator (Mr. T. Saldkeld) to John Lord Boyle, among much heavy rubbifh in the way of ftyle, and rufty allegories, which were the knowledge vehicles then in vogue, there are many gems. And yet, perhaps, one has no right to complain of this circumlocution, for if it were the mere pith of the matter we wanted, the leaft thinking amongft us are, hourly

and daily feeling, acting, and uttering, condenfed
into a proverb, fome one of thofe truths which
are elaborated in, and diffufed over, an effay.
Don Baltafar was evidently a man poffeffing
great practical knowledge of the world, and as
fuch was duly imbued with that great truth,
conftituting the firft principles of focial intercourfe, that—

> Manners make the man, want of them the fellow,
> And all the reft is leather and prunella.

I fhall therefore give, *in extenfo*, his notions
upon this all-important point, as fet forth in a
letter addreffed to his friend DON BARTHOLOMEW
DE MORLANES.

" That maxim, *A manner in all things*, ought to
be, dear Morlanes, one of the firft you fhould
ftudy to practife, fince CLEOBULUS was ranked
amongft the wife men of the firft clafs for only
having taught it. Not to injure that philofopher,
or wrong the judgment of antiquity, that has
honoured him with fo excellent a name, I fhould
think it infinitely more glorious to practife a
thorough regularity and decency of behaviour,
than to teach it in the moft flourifhing academy.
To know how to prefcribe excellent rules, and
nothing more, is to be only a fimple rhetorician ;
but to teach, and to practife what one teaches, is to
be a philofopher in earneft ; *that* entitles one firftly
to the denomination of a philofopher and wife man

in the true fenfe of the words. Be that as it will, *A manner in everything* is one of the acknowledged maxims neceflary in practice ; as there are certain principles allowed as felf-evident in fpeculation. No ; a man fhould never be negligent about the MANNER in any matter whatfoever ; for the MAN-NER is that which is always moft obvious and vifible ; 'tis the outfide, the mark, the fign, and the fpecification, as it were, of the THING. By that external we come to the knowledge of the internal; by the *rine* [rind] and outfide of the fruit, which is vifible to the eye, we conjecture and judge of its nature and quality. A man likewife, whom we never faw in our lives, makes himfelf known to us in fome meafure by his air and his figure. Thus, is a manner fo far from being an indifferent circumftance with refpect to merit, that it is the very thing which notifies it to our fenfes, 'tis that which roufes our attention and engages it towards an object that has already been capable of pleafing us at firft fight. This fort of perfec-tion (for a perfection it is) comes within the reach and capacity of all people,[1] confequently,

---

[1] No, verily, Don Baltafar, it does *not*, for, like poets, they muft be " to the manner *born*." But what *does* come within the reach of all, with care and attention, if they would only put afide their felfifhnefs and doff their felf-conceit, is to be a little lefs ill-bred, by being more mindful of the feelings, or even it may be of the prejudices, of others.

it is unpardonable to renounce it, whatever some pretenders to solidity may allege, who look upon manner as a trifling, inconfiderable circumftance. Some perfons are born with happy difpofitions for the acquiring of this talent, but yet they will never have it in perfection unlefs they themfelves fecond the advances that nature has made in their favour. There are others who have no previous difpofitions towards this talent ; thefe muft remedy that difadvantage by their own induftry ; art will, at leaft in fome meafure, fupply the defect of their natural deficiency. But when Nature in this refpect is feconded by Art and application, from that union will proceed a merit that charms mankind, a *je ne fçay quoy*,[1] an inexpreffible fomething that adorns our actions, beautifies our perfons, and ennobles nobility itfelf. TRUTH indeed has its force, REASON its power, and JUSTICE its authority ; but every one of thefe lofes much of its value if it be not fet off and adorned with a becoming manner, but if they be accompanied by a fuitable manner, how greatly then is their value enhanced ! The charm of manner does yet more : it fupplies the very place of a thing itfelf, and compenfates for the meannefs or defect of it. It gives ftrength to a feeble truth, depth to a fuperficial reafon, and weight to

---

[1] Je ne fais quoi.

an infufficient authority. It even makes us forget
—what do I fay? it actually covers and razes—
that is too little ftill—it graces and adorns the
imperfections of Nature, and makes amends for
the niggard portion fhe has given us. In a word,
MANNER is a kind of univerfal fupply that fur-
nifhes us with every thing we want. How many
affairs have been fpoiled and ruined by a difagreeable manner and behaviour, and how many, on
the other hand, have been profperous and fuc-
cefsful, folely through the advantage of an agreeable deportment!

" The monarch's power, the ftatefman's aftute-
nefs, the general's bravery, the fcholar's learning,
are all imperfect qualities, if they be deftitute of
a fuitably graceful demeanour; but this equivalent,
enhancing attribute (if I may fo exprefs it), becomes a fubftantial, effential perfection, in thofe
perfons who are born to govern, or chofen to
command. Generally fpeaking, all fuperiors gain
more refpect and deference by condefcenfion and
humanity than by demanding or exacting them
in a defpotic or imperious way; and a fovereign
in particular, who fhades his greatnefs with an air
of kindnefs and benevolence, doubly engages us
to do our duty. By that means he reigns in our
hearts, and confequently over all the reft.

" In fhort, Manner is in all conditions and
fituations, an irrefiftible attraction and engage-

ment; it procures good-will at firſt ſight, and
after having made that ſtep, it advances by degrees, and gains eſteem, and by theſe progreſſive
motions it riſes at laſt to encomiums and
applauſe.   We ought, therefore, as I before ſaid,
to omit no means or pains whatſoever, towards
the forming of this talent, if Nature has not im-
planted it in us; for after all, they that are
pleaſed with it (and who is there, that is not?) do
not inquire whether it be natural or acquired;
they reliſh the pleaſure of it, without any further
examination or inquiry.

"MANNER,[1] in regard to the productions of
wit and underſtanding, is almoſt a fundamental
point.   In the firſt place, if any piece of literature be grown antiquated, or ſunk into oblivion
or obſcurity, or neglected and thrown by, from
having been writ by an unſkilful author, this
talent alone will bring it out of that ignominy
and obſcurity into light, with honour and advantage.   It reforms the antique groſſneſs of
ſuch pieces, that would be offenſive to the
modern politeneſs; it trims and dreſſes 'em up
ſo agreeably, that the world receives them with
as much applauſe as if they were new products
of the writer's own genius.[2]   But as we grow

---

[1] *i.e.* Style.
[2] Terrible encouragement (by no means wanted) for
wholeſale plagiariſts, this!

every day more and more perfect, the prefent prevailing tafte, you'll fay, and not the ancient, is to be confulted, to furprife the modern reigning tafte out of a fuperannuated compofition, or old-fafhioned treatife. A fmall alteration is often fufficient for that purpofe, fome little new turn, which difguifes the old thought, and makes it pafs for a new one.[1] Every thing feems to become new in fome men's hands,[2] that have a certain peculiar caft of wit. With that talent they take out all that's flat in a mean author, all that is infipid in a trite fubject, and all that's fervile in an imitation. Let the matter they handle be what it will, hiftorical or rhetorical, the hiftorian will be read and the orator will be heard; for though the fubject may be common, yet 'tis treated after a new and uncommon manner.

---

[1] Indeed! What a pity that this art, like that of painting on glafs, fhould be loft to the prefent generation!

[2] As in thofe of the Mofaic-Arab gentlemen of Monmouth Street or the Minories, for inftance, or as a politician's coat, however often turned, or even what may be called a gilt-gingerbread calibre of intellect, from the grotefque trafhinefs of its fubftratum, plaftered on the furface with an ornate gorgeoufnefs of glitter that amounts to vulgarity, may, with manner and temper combined, vanquifh the fatal Hydra RIDICULE itfelf, which keeps watch and ward at the bafe of Ambition's very dirty flippery *mât de cocagne*, fucceed in climbing it, and vigoroufly feize from its pinnacle the onerous burdens of its golden talifmans of power and pofition.

"In the second place, things that are in themselves choice and exquifite, 'tis true, do not weary us, though they be prefented to our minds over and over again. But yet if they do not weary us, they at leaft ceafe to entertain us with equal pleafure. Now this is the time we fhould perceive it neceffary to have recourfe to the magic of manner, and to give the fubject that new drefs which it feems to require. The new decoration ftrikes and awakens the fancy, and pleafes it as much as if fome new objects were prefented to it ; whereas they are only the fame, placed in a new and different light ; old pictures juft vamped up, and re-varnifhed. Thefe, then, are two maxims conftantly true in matters of literature : that, on the one hand, the moft ingenious piece will not be pleafing to the tafte if it be not feafoned and difhed up with an agreeable manner, and, on the other hand, the moft common or trivial thing is no longer fo, if it be treated in a polite(!) way, in that engaging manner which new-models every thing it takes in hand.

"A manner is likewife of great advantage in civil fociety,[1] in the common, ordinary converfe of life. Let two men relate the fame ftory : the

---

[1] So it is to be prefumed, for without good manners fociety, were it called *la crême de la crême*, can fcarcely *be* civil.

one fhall pleafe, and the other difguft ; this is a
wide difference, whence does it proceed ? Why,
it proceeds entirely from the manner. The one
has fomething in his air and manner that is
either affecting, engaging, humorous, or *piquant,*
the other has fomething awkward or dull in his
perfon and language, which tires the hearers, or
lulls them to fleep. But the worft of all is,
when a man's manner and behaviour is not only
not agreeable, but is pofitively bad and difagreeable, and that wilful and affected too, as is often
the cafe with men in great pofts and employ-
ments. How many have we known whofe
harfh, rude, infolent, brutifh manner has made
all mankind avoid them ! ‘Your haughty, fu-
percilious air,’ faid a wife man once—to one that
you and I know[1]—‘ is not indeed in itfelf a vice
which ought to brand you with difhonour ; but
neverthelefs, it is a fault, and fuch a confiderable

---

[1] The reader will have the goodnefs to bear in mind,
‘‘ *que c'eft Marc Aurèle qui parle, ce n'eft pas moi:* ” it is Don
Baltasar’s pen this philippic emanates from, not mine ; and
that the *you* and *I* here invoked are himfelf and Don Bartholomew de Morlanes. I myfelf—I, gentle reader—have
fpared you not only the battering-rams of *italics* with which
Don Baltafar affaults this official Growley of *his* day, but
even all the capitals (at leaft all thofe of Europe) that he
had crammed into this paffage, to make it the more im-
pregnable and impofing.

fault too, that it alienates all civilized people from you, and banifhes them from your houfe and prefence. Have you a mind to recover and bring back thefe amiable fugitives? do but put on a gracious, obliging air; that attraction alone will bring them all again; for that metamor-phofis and change of the exterior will perfuade them there was firft of all one within.'

"A volume would not be fufficient to par-ticularize all the advantages of an agreeable manner. It intermixes fo many civil things, even in a refufal, that we fcarcely perceive it to be one. At leaft, we take it more kindly than a favour granted us with an ill grace and reluctant countenance. It fo qualifies a reprimand too, that it makes it appear more like an admonition than a reproof. Under a kind approbation of our conduct, which it feems to look upon as difcreet, it will couch and infinuate a genteel(!) remonftrance, finely to point out and intimate to us, that we are not fo perfect as we fhould be. In a word, MANNER is a fort of univerfal fpecific for all diforders,[1] an univerfal fupplement

---

[1] If Don Baltafar be right, *this* quite accounts—defpite our draining and lighting and fanitary improvements—for our ever-increafing bills of mortality; but it's an ill wind (and *not*, it would appear, an ill manner,) that blows nobody any good; and what a paradife England muft be, and *is*, for M.D.s! They have only to make a name, and, like Mofes

to all defects and imperfections, an univerfal means towards an univerfal fuccefs.

"But after all, fay you, what is this manner you fpeak of? in what does it precifely confift? It is, in fhort, a thing not to be defined; for it confifts in a certain *je ne fçay quoi* [*je ne fais quoi*], an indefinable fomething, that cannot be explained either. Without attempting, then, to analyze its nature and effence, I fhall only call it an affemblage, or conjunction of perfections, a mafter-piece of work, finifhed by the hands of all the Graces.

"We need not go back to former ages for an example of this mafterpiece, this inexplicable, inexpreffible, fomething. Ifabella de Bourbon, Queen of Caftile, was poffeffed of this union of perfections, attefted by the general admiration and applaufe of all Spain, not to mention a thoufand other qualities, which gained her more glory than any queen of her name ever merited in this kingdom. This princefs had fuch a charming manner, fuch engaging, winning ways, an affability fo natural, eafy, and yet majeftic, that fhe won the hearts of all who approached her. She did a great deal in a little time. She lived univerfally admired, and died univerfally lamented.

in the "Vicar of Wakefield," to go to fleep. They need fear no rival healers in good manners!

" Heaven foon claimed this angelic vertue [*i. e.*
virtue], of which this world was not worthy.
Ifabella de Bourbon, after having been the too
fhort-lived felicity of this kingdom, was taken
hence to the fruition of an eternal felicity prepared for her merits."

But to return to our own bad manners. I
do maintain that they arife more from intenfe
felfifhnefs than pride, as foreigners fuppofe ; or
rather that pride, the vulgar fungus commonly
fo called, is but the fecondary refult of the firft
principle, felfifhnefs. As one, among many inftances, of the fort of almoft incredibly bad
manners which perfons are fubjected to in this
country in their unavoidable public intercourfe
with their compatriots, I will relate one of which
I was eye and ear witnefs. A fhort time ago,
on a fummer's Sabbath evening, I ftrolled into a
mediæval church to look at the monuments and
painted windows, which during the fervice I had
of courfe been unable to examine. I foon perceived that I was not alone in my explorations,
but that two ladies—I mean LADIES—were fimi-
larly employed. At length, tired by their re-
fearches, they entered a pew near the reading
defk, while I foon after took poffeffion of an
oppofite one. The two ladies upon going into
their feat had knelt down to pray, we three
being the only perfons then in the church.

They had fcarcely concluded their devotions when the firft bell began to toll for evening prayers, and foon after the verger came down the centre aifle, and after having lit the gas at the reading defk, handed them a hymn book, which feemed to endorfe, as it were, their right to the places they had felected, though no doubt they, like myfelf, were under the impreffion that at the evening fervice, whoever came firft were free to take any vacant feat they chofe. All went on fmoothly till towards the end of the Firft Leffon, when two young—*ladies*, I fuppofe they would have called themfelves—but terribly beflowered, befurbelowed and befeathered figures, came ruftling and buftling down the aifle, and, not fpeaking in that low, fubdued tone which inferiors generally adopt before their earthly fuperiors—ftill more in the Houfe of God— they dafhed open (for I can defcribe it in no other way) the pew door where the two ladies fat, and faid in a *loud* voice, "You can't fit here —this is *our* pew."

Now what confiderably added to the *Chriftian* grace of this proceeding was, that there was ample room in the pew for four. The LADIES did not wait for a fecond notice to quit, and opening my pew door for them I betook myfelf to another, not but what there was plenty of room in the one I occupied ; but after the fpecimen of good breeding they had juſt experienced I thought they might prefer being alone.

This accurſed omnipreſence of ſelf is for ever riſing to the ſurface, and tainting and twanging all beneath, like that horrid oil by which the Italians exclude the air (at the expenſe of the flavour of the wine) on the top of their flaſks of Monte Pulciano and Falernian; or that "*Spirate* of Cinnamon," which Algernon Sidney wrote to his friend, Mr. Furley, at the Hague, to get for him, with the warmeſt Indian gown he could find at Amſterdam, adding, touching the *Spirate* :—

"Perhaps you may at the ſame place *heare* of that ſpirate of cinnamon that you ſent me once into France, and I ſhould be glad to have as much more now, if I could have that which is right and good, but I *heare* there is knavery in *that buſineſſe* as well as many others; and the way of ſending the laſt, with *Oile* on the top, was good to preſerve it, but I never found a way ſoe to take it off but it mixed with the *ſpirate* and ſpoilt the taſte and ſmell."

And verily ſo does this rancid oil of ſelfiſhneſs (which is intended as a ſafeguard to the body over which it preſides) "mix with the ſpirit," and ſpoil the flavour and aroma of all other qualities. And the worſt effect of this ſelfiſh-neſs is, that the heart, which God made and intended to be *elaſtic*, is hardened and narrowed into a pſychology of the Greek ſculptor's " Homunculus meaſuring the Coloſſal Statue by its Thumb." Theſe ſelfiſh homunculi meaſure all greatneſs by ſome homœopathic rule of thumb of their own. A large heart, a great mind, and ſtill more, a great nature, *they* cannot underſtand ; and only look upon them as convenient reſervoirs of folly for ſupplying their wants. So that with ſuch perſons, let them be under whatſoever obligations they may to others, decency is difficult, and gratitude impoſſible. For in every way they are as tough and obtuſe as a rhinoceros ; to win them is alſo impoſſible, to offend them is equally ſo ; for their own intereſt, or at leaſt *ends*, being the only thing they keep ſteadily in view, though under ordinary circumſtances their manners may be uncouth and repulſive in the extreme, yet no ſooner is it a queſtion of inſult verſus intereſt than ſtraight they are

" Made all of falſe-faced ſoothing, when ſteel grows
Soft as the paraſite's ſilk."

And oh ! how ſhocked ſuch reptiles are, with their toad-like fibres that can diſpenſe with the very breathing element of other natures, and ſtill drag on their ſlow, cold, marrowleſs exiſtence, how utterly ſcandalized they are, when they have

goaded fome frank, honeft nature, by treachery
and bafe ingratitude, into one of thofe terrific
heart-quakes, where

> " What the breaft forges the tongue muft vent ;
> And being angry, do forget that ever
> They heard the name of death."

For then the *fæva indignatio* reigns fupreme.

Well-bred perfons, whatever inconvenience
they may put themfelves to or facrifices they
may make to ferve another, were it to the amount
of more than half their worldly goods, would of
courfe *leffen* and make light of the favour to the
obligée ; but towards the genuine Anglo-Saxon
this is a moft fupererogatory piece of delicate
generofity, as they are fure to put *that* con-
ftruction on it, and to point it out to you, fo as
in fact to tranfpofe the pofitions, and endeavour
out of your own mouth to prove that *you*, not
they, are the debtor ; for moft perfons, though
by no means too proud to accept any fort of
affiftance, are generally too mean to acknowledge
it.   If out of *fheer* compaffion, at a great facrifice
of perfonal or pecuniary comfort, you give houfe-
lefs and friendlefs perfons a home, though they
may be morally and phyfically everything that
is moft antipathic and obnoxious to you ; when
on the firft opportunity they play you fome
Judas trick, and you are ftung by their bafe

ingratitude into complaining of the bad return
fuch conduct is for the years of kindnefs they
have received from you, the odds are they
tell you " Why, you yourfelf told me that, fo
folitary a life as you led, it was quite an acquifi-
tion to have any one to ftay with you!" or if,
out of the fame foolifh compaffion, you have
allowed fome thoroughly difagreeable and in no
way defirable perfon to infeft your houfe all the
year round, merely becaufe you knew he or fhe
wanted a dinner, and had not the means of pro-
curing it ; and that further, you had adminiftered
to his or her pecuniary neceffities far more largely
than your own warranted—when the turn of the
wheel feparates you, whatever forrows or mif-
fortunes may befall you, though they be not of a
defcription fimilar to thofe you relieved in them,
and though there are pens, ink, paper, and poftal
arrangements all the world over, not one word
of fympathy or remembrance will you receive
from your *friends*, till, perhaps, at the end of
another decade, they may want again a fum of
money ; and not knowing any other fool fo likely
as the former oft-tried one to give it them, *then*
will come a letter faying, " from your many
former profeffions of friendfhip, he or fhe is fure
you will not refufe," but not one fyllable about
or allufion to the many fignal fervices they had
received from you ; the truth of the matter being

that you never had felt or could feel, for so
narrow and fordid a nature, any friendfhip; ftill
lefs had you *profeffed* to do fo, though out of
fheer compaffion for their diftrefs you *had done*
them many fignal fervices. But the *fuppreffio
veri* and *fuggeftio falfi* are infeparable from little
minds and fhallow hearts in *all* things, but
more efpecially where gratitude is due, and being
thoroughly infolvent in that virtue, like other
unprincipled creditors, they prefer fwindling you
by any dirty quibble or chicanery. Not that I
have any pecuniary debtors, for to that fort of
perfon I never lend money, but always give it;
which is a practical illuftration of making a
virtue of neceffity; for as I am very fure it
would never be repaid it is as well to take the
initiative, and by robbing onefelf fave them the
additional fin of defrauding one. Now all this
dearth of proper feeling and good principle is
difgufting and difcouraging in the extreme; not
as regards onefelf individually; for anyone who
does a kind act, be it great or fmall, from a
motive of praife, reward, or gratitude, or indeed
from *any* motive but the ONE golden one enjoined
to us from above, of DOING UNTO OTHERS AS WE
WOULD THEY SHOULD DO UNTO US, deferves
not only ingratitude, but cenfure; but it *is* difcouraging, when one *hears* fo much about the
alchemic power of Progrefs, to find how very,

very little it has yet done towards tranfmuting the
drofs of human nature. Perhaps all this arifes
from our being in a tranfition ftate, wherein the
fine old title of GENTLEMAN is much abufed; indeed, the race of men and women (like that
of children) appears to be extinct; *all* perfons
are ladies and gentlemen nowadays, which may
account for a gentleman or a gentlewoman, in the
fingular number, being fo rare. I only wonder
that maids-of-all-work don't advertife as *ladies* not
objecting to do houfehold work, when a far lower
clafs of perfons, thofe figuring in ftreet brawls and
police reports, tenacioufly infift upon the grade;
for we conftantly read, "the prifoner denied having punched the *lady's* eye or torn her bonnet;
he and *another gentleman* were going along, and
merely afked her the way to Oxford Street." * *
And the other day there was an account of a
poor over-driven bull rufhing into a public-
houfe, where two builders were drinking and
fmoking their pipes in the tap-room; and the
public was informed that after fetting all the taps
of the fpirit-barrels flowing "in its headlong
courfe, the bull rufhed into the tap-room, where
the two *gentlemen* were fmoking," &c.

Speaking of bulls naturally reminds one of
Irifh labourers, the lower order of which are very
witty *gentlemen* indeed, and what is better, have
wit in their anger, and when they meet with a

jauntleman who has no pretenſion to being a gentleman, they know how to repay his ingratitude in his own coin. A happy inſtance of this occurred at a faſhionable watering-place a ſhort time ago. A portly "well-to-do" looking *gentleman* was out boating for his pleaſure in a ſomewhat rough ſea; a ſudden guſt capſiſed the boat, all hands ſtruck out for the ſhore, but the ſtout gentleman, though accuſtomed to keep his head above water all his life, evidently did not know how to ſwim, and in faƈt was in imminent danger, when a poor Iriſhman ſtanding on the eſplanade threw off his coat, jumped into the ſea, and at the riſk of his own life ſaved that of the ſtruggling man, and bore him to ſhore amid the loud cheers of the ſpeƈtators. No ſooner did the *gentleman* in broadcloth find himſelf on *terra firma*, and give himſelf a ſort of Newfoundland-doggiſh ſhake in order to make ſure of his own identity, than, putting his hand into his pocket, he generouſly preſented his deliverer with Sixpence! Pat put it on the palm of his left hand, which he held out at arm's length, and contemplated it in every poſſible light, making the moſt comical face imaginable at it—ſuch as Gulliver may have done at the firſt Liliputian that he ſcrutiniſed in the ſame way—only the Iriſhman ſcratched his head with his right hand the while, till ſuddenly running after the ſtout gentleman, he touched him on the arm with one hand, while between the finger and thumb of the other he tendered him the coin, throwing back his head in a deprecating fort of way, as he faid out loud for every one to hear—

" Here it is, *fur*—I *cudn't*, *indade* I *cudn't*; it would go *agin me* confcience entirely, to take *fich* a fum from yez; for faix! it's *jift* fivepence halfpenny *tree* fardings more *nor* yer worth!"

If roars of laughter could avenge or reward, Pat was amply compenfated and avenged. But the ftout gentleman was faved for the nonce, and to perfons of an habitual and ftony felfifhnefs[1] it never occurs, when an immediate danger or neceffity is once paft, that difafters and dilemmas at all events are conftantly repeating themfelves; and that the rinds of the oranges they have fqueezed and are therefore fo prompt to fling away, may under fome other and future phafe of their career be again ufeful to them. For they do not reflect that in this fhort-fighted ingratitude to its agents it is PROVIDENCE itfelf that they outrage, which may teach them the leffon they fo much require in the fevere fchool of retribution when next fate

---

[1] No doubt fome will exclaim, " But the ftout gentleman's ungrateful conduct arofe from fheer ftinginefs, and not from felfifhnefs or ill breeding." Pardon me, my dear fir or madam; but if *well* analyfed, you will find that *all* meannefs, but more efpecially pecuniary meannefs, is nothing but the hardeft fort of felfifhnefs, or petrified egotifm.

places a fpringe, a pitfall, or a barrier in their way. Alas! fuch natures but too incontrovertibly prove to us that Martial was not far wrong when he afferted that animals are often more generous than the felf-ftyled "paragon of animals," MAN; for they evince on many occafions a fort of humanity where men fhow nothing but brutality, "and if quadrupeds degenerate fometimes on this fcore," adds the poet, "it is only becaufe they are corrupted by the examples of men."

And fo far he is right, for being all the creatures of habit, we are of neceffity influenced and moulded more by example than by precept; and our intenfe felfifhnefs, and the bad manners and ill breeding growing out of them arife from early mifrule, and being allowed to indulge in them in our own families, and where, defpite the *verbal* moral axioms they *hear* (of which even among the leaft virtuous there is never any lack) they are naturally led to practife what they *fee*. For as Lord Bacon truly obferves in one of his ableft effays, that "*Of Cuftome and Education*," "Many examples may be put of the force of *Cuftome*, both upon *Minde* and body. Therefore fince *Cuftome* is the *principall* magiftrate of man's life, let men by all means endeavour to obtain good *Cuftomes*, and certainly *Cuftome* is more perfect when it beginneth in young years."

But it is the little *bienféances* and all-buying and little-cofting amenities of fociety, thofe little things of GREAT IMPORT, the minor morals of life, in which, nationally fpeaking, we are fo lamentably deficient, all of which *lèfe-bienféances* might be eafily avoided if we would make it a rule to fay to ourfelves, "If this were a king, a queen, or any other great perfonage, or one from whom I wanted or expected fomething, or that it was in any way my intereft to pleafe or to con-ciliate, would I thus cavalierly keep them waiting, or break an appointment of my own making? or leave their letter unanfwered? or fhow how much their vifit bored or deranged me? or curtly refufe any requeft they might make me? or *ungracioufly* grant it? or be fo inadvertent as to fay or do the very thing which I was perfectly aware was the thing of all others moft calculated to wound or annoy them?" Confcience could have but one anfwer to this catechifm—an unqualified No!

Then believe me it is wrong fo to act towards our uninfluential equals, doubly wrong if there is anything unjuft and exceptional in their pofition or circumftances, which fhould on that account be given by courtefy the higheft rank, and treated with every deference and confideration. And trebly wrong is this ill-bred remiffnefs towards our focial inferiors and dependants. But when we are guilty of any of these shortcomings we should take heed that the remedy be not worse than the difease—that is, that the apology, from an assumption of patronage and implied superiority, be not more offensive than the original rudeness. For here again our national *gaucherie* and omniprefence of felf generally transposes the positions, and instead of expressing (as common good breeding demands) *their* regret and loss at not having been able to come and see you for so long a time, they generally begin by condoling with *you*, for *your* difappointment in not having seen them, and fearing you must have thought them very unkind. But the worst of these epidemic bad manners is that they are infectious, for it is not in human nature, if too long goaded, to resist the temptation of retaliation, as, like all other animals of better instincts and less reason, we are apt under great provocation to confound retaliation with redress, and so, for the most part, follow the example of the King of Bavaria, who said, when Napoleon I. kept him and several other legitimate royalties waiting for him for a full hour of a bitter cold January day in the carriage at the gates of Malmaifon while he was paying a *sub rosâ* visit to his divorced Josephine: "Puisqu'on nous traite comme des laquais, ma foi! divertons-nous comme tels;"[1]—and forthwith difpatched a real lackey to a neighbouring *cabaret* for bread, cheefe, and wine.

In footh, all bad manners and vulgar reprifals *have* a fpice of the lackey in them.

---

[1] "Since we are treated like footmen, the beft thing we can do is to amufe ourfelves in the fame way as if we really were Knights of the Shoulder-Knot."

SAMUEL PEPYS AND FRANCIS BACON, LORD VERULAM AND VISCOUNT ST. ALBANS.

SAMUEL PEPYS and Lord Bacon: one of the '*littleſt*' and one of the greateſt men who ever lived! "Why, what a jumble!" exclaims the reader, "for even chronologically ſpeaking, Lord Bacon ought to have precedence."

> "True, I grant you, on that ground alone,
> But on none other, as it ſhall be ſhown."

This, the nineteenth century, among many more high-ſounding titles, calls itſelf an age of pro-greſs, but *that* it never can or will be ſo long as mere intellectual ſupremacy continues to paſs current for an all-ſufficient expiation of every ſpecies of moral obliquity and turpitude. Therefore ſhall Francis Lord Bacon, "the brighteſt, wiſeſt, meaneſt of mankind," be weighed in the balance with Samuel Pepys, and be found wanting. Sylla wifely chofe the title of *Felix* rather than that of *Magnus;* we do the very reverfe. The whole ftudy of the age is to be great—not in reality, for that were meritorious, but in appearance; for this is effentially an era of fhams and feemings. However, deduced from the falfe premifes from which we ftart in all things, this is fo far logical, that we *may* be apparently great upon falfe pretences; whereas, in order to be happy, we muft return to firft principles, thofe that we fet before the children in their copy-books; that is, we muft be GOOD. Don't be alarmed; I am not going to give you an elaborate differtation, reader, upon that unknown pagan divinity, fuppofed to be VIRTUE, but as to whofe nomenclature no two heathens, however illuftrious, could ever agree, Ariftotle calling it the glory of humanity; Salluft, the badge of immortality; Seneca, man's only good; Cicero, the root of happinefs; Apuleius, the imprefs of the Deity; Sophocles, inexpreffible riches; Euripides, a rare treafure; Virgil, the beauty of the foul; Cato, the foundation of authority; Socrates, the fountain of felicity; Menander, his buckler; Horace, his ftrength; Bias, his all; Valerius Maximus, a thing ineftimable; Plautus, the price of all things; Cæfar, the perfection of all great qualities; and which,

in the eighteenth century, under the aufpices
of Mr. Samuel Richardfon, culminated in
" Pamela," and was for the firft and laft time
REWARDED!

No, no! if my betters could not break in this
Cruifer of an attribute, fo as that " a child might
ride it," I am not going to attempt it. Why
fhould I, when Socrates, who had the advantage
of living in an age and country where there was
no law of libel, and no periodical prefs nor
Quarterly Reviews, gave it as his opinion that
there was not a man living who thoroughly
underftood anything? If this was the cafe *then*,
when there was fo much lefs to *be* underftood,
and fo many more people to underftand it, (phi-
lofophers included), what Bœotian imbecility it
would be in me, who am a lineal defcendant
from Socrates' majority (limited), to attempt to
analyfe the problematic concrete! I only meant
to fay, and I repeat it, that in order to be happy
we muft be good, and in this at once fimple yet
profound art, Heaven itfelf has condefcended to
be our teacher; for unto every foul born into this
world God has given a moral chronometer, called
confcience, which He has originally fet by his
own great horologe of omnifcience and eternity; if we neglect it, it will run down and be
filent; if we tamper with it, and regulate it
according to falfe computations, it will deceive

both ourfelves and others; but it cannot deceive the Maker, who knows that all its works were perfect when it left His hands; and will demand a ftrict account of the manner in which they have been neglected or perverted.

For which reafon, I fhall proceed to prove that the little, pompous, whilom Secretary of the Admiralty, Samuel Pepys, was, not a better, but certainly *a lefs bad* man than Francis Lord Bacon, Lord High Chancellor of England; *both* having (with fome exceptions, greatly in favour of Pepys) the fame range of vices in perfection. For though a brother chancellor might find that "there was not fo much amifs in my Lord Verulam"[1]—probably becaufe in this age of mouth amenity and moral turpitude, it is part of the *arcana cana* of our fyftem of popular fallacies to confider it *contra bonos mores* to breathe a *word* againft a predeceffor (however remote), or indeed

---

[1] All Mr. Hepworth Dixon's apotheofis of Lord Bacon (publifhed fince this was written) goes to prove is, that bribery, corruption, and felf-feeking were more openly and honeftly carried on in thofe days than they are now, and that my Lord Verulam was no worfe than his contemporaries—only managed ugly bufineffes more cleverly. The worft thing againft him is the *primâ facie* evidence; for it is a villainous countenance, fuch a one as Lavater would have paffed the fame fentence upon that he did on Mirabeau: "You have every vice, and have done nothing to check them."

to fpeak the truth about any one, or any thing, if it can be poffibly avoided—yet any graduate of a ragged fchool well up in his Catechifm and the Ten Commandments would be inclined to hold a different opinion of my Lord Bacon. Of courfe, no one cognizant of the economy, not to fay parfimony of Nature, in the production of real greatnefs and fuperiority, whether in the moral, animal, vegetable, or mineral kingdoms, is fo unreafonable as to expect that John Bramftones fhould grow upon every bramble—that righteous judge of Charles I.'s time, whom hiftorians concur in telling us " popularity could never flatter into anything unfafe, nor favour bribe to anything unjuft," ftill there are degrees in everything, and there is, moreover, fuch a thing as wearing one's vices, like one's rue, " with a difference."

Having given Mr. Pepys the *pas* in the firft inftance, I fhall continue to do fo, making a little hieroglyphical fum in addition (as he himfelf might have done) of his merits and demerits and thofe of Lord Bacon ; fetting down 1 whenever the balance is in favour of the Secretary, and 0 when it is againft the Chancellor.

PEPYS.

Pepys kept a Diary or Confeffional, and open confeffion is good for the foul.

In that diary, with unexampled candour, and to fave that celeftial fecretary, the recording angel, trouble at the Day of Judgment, he pithily gives his motives for refufing a tempting bribe that had been offered him to do a little dirty work.

" For I did not think them fafe men to receive fuch a gratuity from, and that I might have it in my power to fay I *had* refufed it."

The mean, felfifh motives for this right conduct are fhared by thoufands of highly refpectable individuals. The unflinching honefty of voluntarily acknowledging them is perhaps UNIQUE.

Pepys, as we have feen, did not take bribes ; and inftead of hypocritically anathematizing all who were guilty of that iniquity, he honeftly, if not exactly nobly (!) tells us *why* he did not do fo ; at all events, he avoided the committal of the fin, though neither purity nor principle had anything to do with his integrity. But on the very rare occafions that cowardice makes men act honeftly, it is hard that the trembling monitor fhould not receive its meed of praife. Neither did Pepys delude and betray his fuitors. On the contrary, he fpent much time in figning pardons gratis, as was proved by the following

BACON.

Lord Bacon did not. *He* was wifer (in his generation), and wrote pompous effays denunciatory of his own efpecial vices.

o

My Lord Verulam invariably took bribes with *both* hands — that is, from his client and his client's adverfary—and whichever bribe weighed the heavieft furnifhed him with the moft weighty reafons for *legally* deciding in favour of the donor. Yet hear how this intellectual Janus, this judicial Judas, *wrote* upon this very iniquity of bribery :—

o

*   *   *   *   *

" The Vices of *Authority* are chiefly *foure* :— *Delaies* ; *Corruption* ; *Roughnefs* ; and *Facilitie*. For *Delaies* give eafie acceffe ; keepe times appointed. Go through with that that is in hand ; and interlace not bufineffe, but of neceffity. For *Corruption* ; *Do not only bind thine own hands from taking, but alfo thy fervants' hands from taking, but bind the hands of futours* [*fuitors*] *alfo from offering* [!] *For integrity ufed doth the one ; but integrity profeffed, and with a manifeft deteftation of* BRIBERY [!!] *doth the other. And avoid not only the fault, but the fufpicion.*" !!!

(As my Lord Bacon evidently thought he was cleverly doing by this impious hypocrify !)

Brought
over
2

comment in his " Diary " on this philanthropic expenditure of his time : " I got nothing for it, which did trouble me much." *Anglicè*, like many more, he had much trouble for nothing. *Poverino* Pepys!

1

THE TWO CLOAKS.

Pepys also combined loyalty with economy, and if he often evinced the spirit of his father the tailor, he invariably eschewed the *goose*, where his own pocket and person were concerned. So the Diary has the following very sensible entry, which was no doubt the aboriginal "COMBINING ELEGANCE WITH ECONOMY" now so common in tailors' advertisements :—

" I did countermand the making of my velvet cloak for a time, till I should see which way the queen's illness did issue."

(Mem.) Pepys had never received any honours or emoluments from Charles II.'s queen, as Lord Bacon had done from Elizabeth.

1

Pepys, on the contrary, never betrayed or did anything to injure *his* patrons, my Lord Sandwich or the king; but on the contrary, was remarkably civil and *prévenant* always to their respective "Misses," as honorary wives were in those days called. And upon once being pressed

BACON.

" *Whosoever is found Variable, and changeth manifestly, without manifest cause, giveth suspicion of Corruption.*"

(For which reason my Lord Verulam never *changed*, for he never *decided* till he knew he had good and *sufficient* reasons for his decision.)

IN HYPOCRISY FIVE HUNDRED FATHOMS BELOW PEPYS.

OOOOO

THE TWO CLOAKS.

When on the 23rd of March, 1602, the day before Queen Elizabeth died, my Lord Verulam took water at Whitehall to go down to Richmond "to inquire how long the Queene's Highnesse was like to last, he chid his serving man for giving him his best cloake,—when neither the queene, nor the weather, were like to hold out. On getting to Richmond he met Dr. Whitgift, the Archbishop of Canterbury, who told him the Queene had just commanded her coronation ring, which had grown into the flesh, to be filed off her finger: and the almonds of her ears having begun to swell and an universal numbness to seize her. She was far on her last journey. The rain now beginning to come down, my Lord hasted back to his barge, well pleased that he had had more forethought than his

Brought
over

4

PEPYS.

to cook certain accounts he flatly refufed, as the Diary tells us, "from fear, and from unwillingnefs to wrong the king; and *becaufe it was no profit to me*" [!] Here is Truth again, in her anti-crinoline coftume, drawn up out of her well, and the parifh beadle and county gaol on active fervice, *vice* confcience and honour, promoted. Then Pepys, though he was always making effays on love, never wrote one; and whether we contemplate him being fpat upon at "the play-houfe" by a lady, and not minding it when he found fhe was pretty, or getting up an ecftafy at the fight of Lady Caftlemaine's "*laced fmock as it did hang out to dry,*" or giving "Nym" £5, when he only gave Mrs. P— £2, as will fometimes happen in the beft regulated familics, he was always the greateft gallant poffible in a fmall way.

I

Pepys carried always about him in his beft coat pocket, and did not care to fhare its contents with any one fo long as it contributed to his own perfonal comfort, a fmall homœopathic cafe of poifonous globules of the moft infinitefimal variety, which he took regularly and felt quite comfortable, even to thinking when he was in his own beft Niagara of a wig, with its cataracts of curls, that in *défhabille* the king was but a poor

Bacon.

ſervitors, not to waſte *a faire cloake on foule weather !"*   ○

My Lord Verulam, having too great a mind for   ○
ſo lowly and humble a virtue as gratitude to take
root in, *prudently* betrayed his too generous friend,
patron, and benefactor, Eſſex, thinking, no doubt,
that for a genius with ſuch a head as his, a
friend's head was as good a ſtepping-ſtone as any
in the court of ſo profligate, heartleſs, and un-
womanly a ſovereign as Elizabeth.   What a
pity it is that he did not *leave to the world, and
after a while to this country*, an eſſay on Gratitude
as well as that on " Love !" as it would, there is
little doubt, have been well worthy of the man
who wrote : " It is a poor ſaying of Epictetus—
Satis magnum alter, alteri theatrum ſumus—as if
a man, made for the contemplation of Heaven
and all noble objects had nothing to do but
kneel before a little Idoll and make himſelfe ſubject, though not of the mouth (as Beaſts are), yet
of the eye, which is given for higher purpoſes !"   ○

Lord Bacon's ſelf-valuation was allopathic
and coloſſal, and he purpoſely bequeathed it to
the world as an all-ſufficient portion.   The ſtu-
pendous brilliancy of ſuch an intellect, in the
midſt of ſo low and miry a moral organization,
may be compared to a Bude light in a charnel

Pepys.

looking fellow, though when filked and fatined he
looked noble. Pepys, with all his little Liliputian
pompofity, never hypocritically pointed out the
right way to others; he only took care to go by
it himfelf, *not* from the glorious immortality promifed at the end of it—for he had no fuch lofty
afpirings — but becaufe he dreaded the fnares,
fpring guns, and foul things that might bemire
his fine clothes, or even the cafualties that might
ftrip him of them altogether, if, tempted by a
fhort cut, he took a wrong turn.

BACON.

houfe, illuminating in all its loathfomenefs the corruption it could not purify. He *knew* what was right, and pointed it out to others, not indeed from a laudable wifh for their welfare, but to put them by hypocrify on a wrong fcent ; and while indicating to them the beft road, prevent their perceiving the crooked and foul ways by which he himfelf travelled.[1]

---

[1] But all this is only a proof how well my Lord Verulam underftood and practifed his own axioms on "*vaine glory*," which are fo perfectly underftood and carried out alfo in our own times. "In fame of learning," faith he, "the flight will be flow without fome feathers of *Oftentation. Qui de contemnendâ Gloriâ libros fcribunt, Nomen fuum infcribunt.* SOCRATES, ARISTOTLE, GALEN, were men full of *oftentation.* Certainly *vaine glory* helpeth to perpetuate a man's memory; and Vertue was never fo beholding to Humane Nature, as it received its due at the fecond hand. Neither had the Fame of *Cicero, Seneca, Plinius Secundus,* borne her age fo well, if it had not bin joined with fome *vanity* in themfelves. Like unto varnifh, that maketh feelings [ceilings] not only to fhine, but laft." All of which, though elaborately practifed now, was condenfed in the Syrian proverb fome thoufands of years ago, "Give yourfelf *one* ear-ring of gold, and the world will foon give you the other."

Brought
over
OOOOOO
OOO

OOOOOO
OOOOOO

Having now fhown, what Lord Bacon himfelf would have called "A TABLE OF THE COLOURS OR APPEARANCES OF GOOD AND EVILL, AND THEIR DEGREES, AS PLACES OF PERSWASSION AND DISWASION, AND THEIR SEVERAL FALLAXES AND THE ELENCHES OF THEM," between the pigmy and the giant, it is clearly proved, by moral gauge, which is God's meafure and the only one we fhall be judged by hereafter, although it is quite the reverfe *here*, that although with regard to their fmall vices it is fix of one and half-a-dozen of the other, between the Chancellor and the fecretary, yet morally fpeaking the balance is in favour of the latter; Samuel Pepys being on the *fame* fcores fix times a lefs bad man than FRANCIS LORD BACON. The how, when, and wherefore, of this great famenefs, yet great difference, in the *modus operandi* of fimilar vices in two individuals created out of fuch widely different argils and in antipodical fpiritual and intellectual hemifpheres, muft be left to metaphyficians to determine.

Dr. Clarke and Wollafton confidered moral obligation as arifing from the effential difference and relations of things; Shaftefbury and Hutchefon as arifing from the moral fenfe; and the generality of divines as arifing folely from the will of God. On thefe three principles practical morality has been built. "Thus has God been

pleafed," adds Warburton, "to give three different
excitements to the practife of virtue, that men of
all ranks, conftitutions, and educations might find
their account in one or other of them,—fomething that would hit their palate, fatisfy their
reafon, or fubdue their will. But this admirable
provifion for the fupport of virtue hath been in
fome meafure defeated by its pretended advocates,
who have facrilegioufly untwifted this threefold
cord."

Exactly fo, and this brings us to the great and
infoluble problem of why it fo often happens that
the cleareft and loftieft intellects, as in the inftance
of Lord Bacon, are found linked with the very
bafeft moral obliquities. This, truly, is the
Mezentian punifhment, of the dead body bound
and chained to the living one, fpiritualized, and
perpetuated on into an inexorable eternity. Such
men, who have for the moft part but a fmall
worldly ambition, even to achieve *that* play the
wrong card; for nothing in heaven or earth has
any vitality in it fave *goodnefs—not* the *appearance*
but the REALITY.

If God Himfelf were merely great it is very
probable that we fhould even be *afraid* to pray
to Him; Omnipotence may will, and in willing
awe; Omnifcience may know, and with the fubtle
myfteries of fuch infinite knowledge work miracles; but it is GOODNESS alone which can fave

or attract, for Goodnefs is the heart of Time and the foul of Eternity. When we appeal to God it is *not* His power we invoke; on the contrary, we often dread that; but it is to his GOODNESS we pray, and to *that* we TRUST.

If the *manes* of the departed are cognizant of the phantafmagoria going on in this world after they have paffed the great Rubicon, and ftill more, if they can either gladden or wince under the pofthumous verdicts of their fellow men, I cannot imagine my Lord Verulam's punifh-ment having reached its grand climacteric, or his myriads of defrauded clients being appeafed, till he found himfelf coupled with Samuel Pepys, and even lofing by the comparifon!

Notwithftanding this *Fiat juftitia*, however, I feel bound to return my grateful thanks for the many pleafant hours I have paffed with my Lord Bacon, more efpecially in his "Gardens," wondering the whiie when he talked fo much of DEW-BAYES yielding fuch fweet odours of a morning, "GERMANDERS,[1] that give fuch good flower to the eye," with "CORNELIANS," and

---

[1] Doubtlefs the "PRIME-ROSES" mentioned fo often, and with befitting praifes, by Lord Bacon, were merely the an-ceftors of our own little darling meadow-ftars the Primrofes, and, like all other names, theirs was originally beftowed to defignate a peculiarity or a quality, that of their being the firft rofes of the year.

for fruits, of " GINNITINGS," "QUADLINGS,"
and " MELO-COTONES "—I could not help wondering, I fay, the while, what and where they
were; though I could perceptibly inhale the perfume of the dainty mufk-rofes, that of the woo-
ing white violets, and the fpicy tufted pinks,
in all directions.

For the benefit of a certain clafs of young
ladies who may not have read his " Effaies," from
thinking Bacon vulgar in any fhape, I will leave
the "Gardens" and return into the " Buildings,"
and go into that " *Goodly Roome above ftaires of fome
forty feet high*," or rather into the fmall *fanctum*
next to it, on "*the houfehold fide*," and take from
under a heap of parchments that little fquare
booke with its red edges, bearing date 1597, being
the firft edition of thofe wonderful " Effaies," and
read you one of the quainteft, that "OF MASQUES
AND TRIUMPHS," (xxxvii.)—merely afking by
the way, what would be thought of a Lord
Chancellor in the year of grace 1876, who wrote
upon operas and ballets, merely becaufe the
Queen *would* have fuch gauds, and being the
keeper of her Majefty's confcience he thought it
his duty to look after the *coryphées* ?

Of Masques and Triumphs.

THESE things are but Toyes, to come amongst such serious observations, but yet, since Princes will have such things, it is better they should be Graced with Elegancy, than Daubed with cost.—*Dancing to Song*, is a thing of great State, and Pleasure. I understand it, that the song be in Quire[1] placed aloft, and accompanied with some broken Musicke: And the Ditty fitted to the Divice. *Acting in Song*, especially in *Dialogues*, hath an extreme Good Grace: I say *Acting*, not *Dancing :* (for that is a mean, and vulgar Thing ;) And the *Voyces* of the *Dialogue* should be strong and manly (a Base, and a Tenour, no Trebble) And the *Ditty* High, and Tragicall ; Not nice, or Dainty. *Severall quires*, placed one over against another, and taking the voyce by Catches, *Antheme* wise, give great Pleasure. *Turning dances* into *figure*, is a childish Curiosity.—And generally let it be noted, that those Things, which I here set downe, are such as do naturally take the sense, and not respect petty wonderments. It is true the alterations of scenes, abound with *Light*, specially coloured, and varied : And let the Masquers, or any other, that are to

---

[1] Choir.

come downe from the Scene, have some Motions
upon the *Scene* itselfe, before their Comming
downe, For it drawes the Eye strangely, and makes
it with great pleasure, to see, that, it cannot perfectly discern.—Let the *Songs* be *Loud* and Cheere-
full, and not *Chirpings*, and *Pulings*. Let the
Musicke likewise be *Sharpe* and loud (!) and well
placed. The *Colours* that shew best by Candle
light, are ; White, Carnation, and a kinde of Sea-
water-Greene ; and *Ols*, or Spangs,[1] as they are
of no great cost, so they are of most Glory [!] ; as for
rich *Embroidery*, it is lost and not Discerned. Let
the *Sutes* of the Masquers be Gracefull, and such
as become the person, when the Vizars are off.
Not after examples of known attires ; Turkes,
Souldiers, Mariners, and the like. Let *Anti-
masques* not be long ; they have been commonly of
Fooles, Satyres, Baboons, Wilde-Men, Antiques,
Beasts, Spirits, Witches, Ethiopes, Pigmies, Tur-
quets [?], Nimphs, Rusticks, Cupids, Statuas,
Moving, and the like. As for Angels,—it is not
comicall enough [!] to put them in *Anti-masques*,
and any thing that is hideous, as Devils, Giants,
is on the other side, as unfit : But chiefly let the
Musicke of them be Recreative, and with some
strange changes. Some *Sweet Odours* suddenly
coming forth, without any drops falling, are in

---

[1] *i.e. Oripeaux* and spangles.

such a Company, as there is Steame and Heat, Things of great Pleasure, and Refreshment. *Double Masques*, one of them, another of Ladies, addeth State and Variety. But all is nothing, except the *Roome* he kept Cleare, and Neat. For *Justs, Turneys,*[1] and *Barriers;* the Glories of them are chiefly in the Chariots, wherein the Challengers make their Entry; especially if they be drawne with Strange Beasts; as Lions, Bears, Camels, and the like; or in the Devices of their Entrance, or in Bravery of their Liveries; or in the Goodly Furniture of their Horses, and Armour. But enough of these Toyes."

I think so too; but *Cede magnis !*

---

[1] *i.e.,* Jousts and tourneys.

FORGIVE AND FORGET.

WHOEVER firſt linked they twain to-gether in "holy matrimony" knew human nature *well;* as forgetting is the ſynonyme of forgiving. Till we *do* forget we cannot forgive. It muſt be an unchriſtian ſpirit indeed that would not forgive even the moſt irremediable injuries, *if aſked to do ſo,* coupled with an aſſurance of ſincere regret, on the part of the aggreſſor. But there are ſome natures ſo Phariſaical and mean, that their *modus operandi* is always to merge a leſſer outrage in a greater. This is ſheer folly, ſo far as the attempts at impunity of ſuch evil-doers are concerned ; for there can be no ſuch thing as willing martyrs where the faggot and the fire are *alone* provided and the crown is withheld ;—as to appeal to a perſon's generoſity is one thing (and with gene-rous natures, to appeal to it is to obtain it), but to ſwindle them out of it by ſnares and ſubterfuges

is another, and the fure way to render oblivion
impoffible. For would God Himfelf forgive us,
if, inftead of afking His forgivenefs in a humble
and contrite fpirit, we on the contrary tried to
fhift all the onus of our fins upon Him, faying
that if HE had not created us or put temptation in our way we fhould not have tranfgreffed;
and that therefore He muft clearly perceive, that
he owed *us* great reparation, for having allowed
our fins to find us out, and bear the bitter fruit
of punifhment which we ourfelves had planted.
And yet there are many fuch inverfe natures, fo
warped by falfe pride and low cunning, that
they invariably tranfpofe the pofitions, and arraign
their victims for the peril *they* have entailed upon
them, whenever detection follows crime; which
is precifely the fame fpecies of inverted logic
reforted to by a certain highwayman in George
the Firft's time; who, upon finding himfelf for the
fecond time in the dock at the Old Bailey, put
his arms akimbo, and knitting his brows and
looking the judge full in the face, faid in a loud
bullying voice, fo that the whole court might
hear it.——

"Harkee, my lord! *this* is the fecond time
I have ftood in this dock; if I find myfelf here a
third time I fhall bind you over to keep the
peace, fwearing you have put me three times in
fear of my life."

But so indispensable is this Lethean process to forgiveness that with the ungratefully treacherous or the criminally weak, who yield to or connive at the misdeeds of others, against their own better natures, we often find,—that it is part of the inscrutable subtlety of God's chemistry of retribution that *they cannot forget*, and consequently *cannot forgive themselves.* Thus Judas flung down the thirty pieces of silver, and went out and hanged himself, thereby acting as his own judge and executioner. And Suetonius mentions that shortly after the Crucifixion, Tiberius deprived Pontius Pilate of his office, and the ex-procurator retired to Vienna ;[1] where, falling into a profound melancholy, he committed suicide.

While then forgiveness of injuries depends so entirely upon the oblivion of them, there are some injuries so chronic, concrete, and ubiquitous, that they are incorporated with not only every SOURCE but with every CHANNEL of our existence, and therefore we must forget *it*, before we can forgive *them*. Moreover, it is an incontrovertible truth, that " Pardon to the injured doth belong ;" therefor is it that evil-doers, that is, aggressors, are always so implacably irate at their victims, putting their deeds into words, and inveigh amain against that English

---

[1] Vienne, in Gaul (France).

focial, literary, and political Bogie—their " ftrong language," while the poor victims can but retort, with Electra in the iambics of Sophocles,

> " *You* do the deeds, and your unholy deeds find *me* the words."

What then is to be done, fince oblivion is the only feed from which forgivenefs can fpring, but one thing : pray to God, to give us that forgetful-nefs which will enable us, not merely in words, but in truth and in fpirit, to forgive thofe who have chronically and irreparably injured us? And oh! what a bleffed anchor is it, in life's moft devaftating ftorms, to the beft as well as to the worft amongft us, to remember that even that great omnipotent God of Mercy was once alfo A Man of Sorrow !

PITY.

IT would appear from the following paragraph, which I read the other day in a newfpaper, and indeed from feveral other little inftances that one meets with in life, that Pity—that gentle dew of human kindnefs, which frefhens and fertilifes all upon which it refts,—like money, generally goes to thofe who don't deferve it. Take the following example :—

"There are in Egypt three hundred miles of railroad. When the running of the trains was commenced MUMMIES were ufed for fuel, and are faid to make a very hot fire. The fupply is almoft inexhauftible, and they are ufed by the cord. What a deftiny !"

What a deftiny indeed! For if the mummies retain a *fpice* of fentiment, if it has not been all *pitched* out of them by time, tombs, pyramids, pedantry, and one thing or another,

they muft be charmed to find themfelves not only
fuddenly called upon to be ufeful to other
fleepers, whom they never dreamt of, but alfo to
think that

"Still in their afhes glow their wonted fires."

But Pity being the theme, fhe really might beftow a tear to think how inanimate, infentient
things, ever outlaft, in this little material planet
of ours, the living, breathing, high-afpiring heirs
of immortality, whofe vaffals and gauds they are
for a brief fpace. I have been led to this reflection by the revelations of Egypt, which are
likely to beat M. de Cuftine's "Revelations of
Ruffia" quite out of the field. Monfieur de
Mariette, another Frenchman, has difcovered in
one of the tombs of the Egyptian kings the
jewel-box of one of Egypt's queens, which, with
its contents, is now the admiration of elegant
and artistic Paris, where even Oberon's and
Titania's choiceft marts for *bijouterie* and knickknackery have long been eftablifhed, and where the
fhades of Benvenuto Cellini and Afcanio might
revel as in a bright little Elyfium of their own.
Well, even *there* is this Egyptian cafket, with
its carcanets, creating boundlefs admiration from
their elaborate workmanfhip and exquifite finifh,
which the perfectionifed art of the prefent day
could not furpafs, either in defign or execution.

Among other things is a small regal crown, cu-
riously wrought in fine gold, and a thick gold
chain six feet long! Think of *that*, ye alder-
men of England, who eat turtle and green peas!
think of it, I say, *even* if, as the French dra-
matist so sublimely and historically expresses it,
there *does*

   "*Coule dans vos veines le plus* NOBLE *sang d'Angleterre*,"
Et que
   "*Votre bisaïeul a été même* DEUX *fois Lord Maire!*"

In this Egyptian queen's jewel-box there is no
mention made of any large pearls (or " unions,"
as they used to be called,) being found. Perhaps
Cleopatra dissolved the last? For in Egypt and
in those barbaric times such matters might have
been considered regal luxuries, but in England,
in this enlightened age, when everything is for
the million, unions are dissolved in vinegar daily,
or permanently, as the case may be, by the
Divorce Court, which enacts, not exactly the
Antony, but the antidote, on such occasions.

But though there were no pearls in the casket,
there was a token of that other priceless pearl in
life's bitter cup—LOVE! which, until it *is* dissolved, converts the very bitterest into nectar.
For there was amid this treasure-trove a beau-
tifully chiselled gold plate or medallion, with a
man's portrait upon it, it is supposed, the portrait
of the king, or at all events of the monarch of

its quondam owner's affections, and this, the
fragile trinket of some gala hour, is now all that
remains of the imperial archives of that queenly
heart, the only vestige of that great world of love it
then reigned over. And yet—no; transition is *not*
death. All other passions may be mortal, and
to be returned to the King of kings at our de-
mise, as the insignia of various orders of knight-
hood are returned to earthly sovereigns, to be
bestowed upon others who succeed us. But
Love is the nucleus of eternity, *the* subtle all-
pervading fluid of that mysterious concrete of
immortality of which each human portion is a
Soul.

It may, nay, it *must* change, but it *cannot* die.
The light of heaven, the breath of flowers, the
song of birds, the summer air, the smile of hope,
the sigh of memory, are each and all full to
over-flowing of it. We see it, hear it, breathe it,
in all things; whether it be in storm or in sun-
shine, in pleasure or in pain, it is *still there*,—
omnipresent, for it is the atmosphere of God's
creation; and who can say then that the Egyptian
queen may not even now be SITTING IN CASSIO-
PEA'S CHAIR, LOOKING THROUGH A MYRIAD
STARRY EYES STILL FONDLY DOWN UPON HER
CHERISHED LOVE GIFTS OF LONG LONG AGO!

ON THE GRATITUDE WE OWE OUR ENEMIES.

IT was a pithy saying that of Lorenzo de' Medici, and true as pithy, that we are enjoined to forgive our enemies, but nowhere are we told that we fhould forgive our friends. One thing is certain, that even our moſt inveterate and moſt influential enemies could prevail but little againſt us (fo invariably does unfcrupulous malice defeat itſelf), but for the treachery, collufion, cowardice, weaknefs, or imbecility of our nominal friends! Therefore we owe this debt of gratitude to our enemies (and it is not a fmall one), that they have been the means of our difcovering the vipers that we have unconfcioufly been warming at our hearths, or worfe ſtill, it may be, in our bofoms, before they had the power of injuring us further. Appeal to any one's experience, and he will tell you that he has largely (that is, with fo few exceptions as

to eſtabliſh the rule), proved the truth of Roche-
foucault's maxim, " Faire un bienfait, faire un
ingrat ;" and yet, as in the vegetable and mineral
kingdoms there grows an antidote near every
poiſon, ſo in the moral world are there innumerable
antidotes to this moſt deadly of all poiſons, ingratitude, even in the immenſity of unſuſpected,
gratuitous, unalloyed, and therefore almoſt ſublime
goodneſs, that exiſts up and down and round
about the world. For ſeldom does any flagrant
inſtance of baſeneſs or ingratitude befall us, but
the reaction of the blow ſtrikes at other hearts that
we ignored till then, and ſets the unſealed foun-
tains of their ſympathy and ſenſe of outraged juſtice guſhing towards us in a thouſand acts of kindneſs and devotion. For no tittle of God's word
ever fails, and thus is His promiſe fulfilled, that if
we caſt our bread upon the waters, after many
days it ſhall return to us. But to convince us of
our own weakneſs and His ſtrength, it generally
does return to us at times and places where we
could have leaſt hoped for it, or rather where we
moſt deſpaired of it. When the neceſſity is at
the greateſt and the ſpirit at the fainteſt, *then*
comes the miraculous bread in the wilderneſs,
WHICH, OUT OF HUMAN IMPOSSIBILITIES, NOT
ONLY SUPPLIES OUR WANTS, BUT EXCEEDS THEM.

A CURIOSITY OF LITERATURE NOT MENTIONED BY ISAAC D'ISRAELI.

THERE are few more charming books in the language for a fireſide companion than D'Iſraeli's "Curioſities of Literature." Still a man cannot read everything, any more than he can know everything. And moreover, thoſe cocks of the walk in literature may be the very antipodes of the chanticleer celebrated by Æſop. *They* may *only* care for gems, and deſpiſe grains of barley, whereas fortunately for you, friend reader, I'm not proud, and therefore much more reſemble the other feathered agriculturiſt in the fable, from infinitely preferring (where a good laugh is the deſideratum) a barley grain, a rogue in grain, or in ſhort anything, to a gem; for there is a brilliancy and intrinſic value about all gems which preclude the poſſibility of laughing at them. But before I hoſpitably and generouſly invite you to ſhare with me,

dear reader, the particular and fomewhat curious
grain of barley upon which I happen to be feafting
at this time, I'll tell you exactly where I was fortunate enough to fcratch it up. Premifing that
in confequence of the prefent democratic movement and tendency to fufion of claffes, I don't fee
why affes fhould not be occafionally ftall-fed, poor
things! as well as oxen, and therefore, I own it, *I*
for one, am much addicted to old book ftalls.
Shallow people, that is, moft perfons, often exprefs
their wonder, that fleek, civilized, gentlemanlike,
well bred, well fed dogs, fhould be fo fond of
poking about, and excavating from ineffable gar-
bage all forts of old bones and fragments in their
walks; aye, and even little pampered, petted,
affected, fine lady, filken-pawed, velvet-eared Blen-
heims and King Charlefes, have to a fpeckle, the
fame *canimania ;* but never (though bleft with a
tolerable good library at home) do I find myfelf
before a ftall covered with old dog-eared, dilapi-
dated looking books,—fome with fhining, dark,
gingerbread-looking covers, others in old emboffed
gold-paper ones, others in parchment that had
once been white, till done brown by that fwindler,
Time, but looking dropfical withal, as if from too
deep potations at the Pierian fpring, and others
with no covers at all,[1]—that I do not perfectly

---

[1] In one of my ftall *bones,* to wit, " A Dissertation on

understand the physiology (perhaps I ought to say the philomathy) of the whole affair. For in wistfully eyeing these old bones of literature I feel, with the dogs, that what others once feasted upon may perchance still contain some scraps worthy either of a dog's nose or a man's notice; though both in the canine and the critical research, it cannot be denied that there intermingles a great deal of Dr. Johnson's definition of a second marriage,—namely, " The triumph of hope over experience." However, the identical grain of barley that we are now about to discuss was not so much sought out by me as that it fell in my way. For in a box of books I received lately was a catalogue of old and second-hand volumes; in spelling

READING THE CLASSICS, and Forming a Just Style: addressed to The Right Honourable JOHN LORD Roos, the Present DUKE OF RUTLAND. By HENRY FELTON, D.D. Printed by Jonah Bowyer, at The Rose, in St. Paul's Church Yard, 1723," is the following instruction to *book keepers, printed* in a square black frame, under the armorial bearings of its former owner, one Mr. Christopher Toogood, and for *this* "Caution to Sinners" it was I bought the volume :—

> The first thing you ought
> to do, when you borrow a
> Book, is, to read it; that
> you may *return* it as soon
> as possible TO THE OWNER.

it over, I was irrefiftibly attracted by the title of
the one I am about to lay before you, *not in extenfo*,
for *that* would be no joke, but a heavy infliction.
And when I received this precious volume it fo
far furpaffed my moft fanguine expectations, both
as to matter and manner, that I inftantly had it
bound in a moft confpicuous manner, fo as that
every one coming in could not fail to notice it; for
it is far too good and unique to be facrificed to
any individual monopoly. Even the author's
name is unique and pre-Adamitifhly original, for
I not only never heard it before, but never heard
a name at all refembling it. But let it and its
owner fpeak for themfelves; and to begin at the
beginning, here is the title-page :—

" Young Gentleman and Lady's Privàte[1] Tutor.
In Three Parts. The Firft Part contains a Preliminary Difcourfe on Moral and Social Duties,
&c., viz. Piety, Wifdom, Prudence, Fortitude,
Juftice, Temperance, Love, Friendfhip, Humanity, &c. The Second Part contains Rules for behaving Genteel [!] in all Stages of Life, of Behaviour to God, Parents, Company, Brothers, Sifters,
Superiors, Equals, Inferiors, Teachers, Servants,
in Company, at Meals, at Cards, &c. Walking

---

[1] No doubt the accent over the à in " privàte " is according
to the author's ideas, to denote the *genteel* way of *publicly*
pronouncing this egotiftical and unfociable word.

alone, With Company, &c. The Third Part
contains Behaviour in the Dancing School, with
Directions for Dancing a Minuet, Walking,
Standing, Giving, Receiving, Bowing, and to make
a Curtfey, &c. To which is added a Set of Figures
of young Gentlemen and Ladies, adapted to the
above Rules. Alfo Habits proper for Gentlemen
and Ladies when Dancing, with Rules, and
Cautions: and Figures fetting forth the true
Ufe of the Fan. By Matthew TOWLE, Dancing
Mafter, in Oxford. Printed for the Author,[1]
MDCCLXX. Sold by J. Fletcher in Oxford;
J. Fletcher in London; and by the Author's
Father and Brother at all the Schools they attend."

> Then afk, "What's in a name?" indeed!
> Oh, fophiftry moft foul!
> Shakefpeare, could even *you* have lived
> If *your* name had been TOWLE?

Mr. Towle next proceeds to find great fault
with the artift who furnifhed the plates for his
valuable work; and not without reafon, I think,
for as he juftly obferves, thefe faid plates are
completely *difhed*, from a ftrange (but ftill perfectly original) defect in the anatomy of the
figures and the perfpective of the inanimate

---

[1] This was, perhaps, a fupererogatory announcement, except as it additionally tends to prove that in no fingle particular
has the uniform and fingular originality of this production
been departed from.

objects reprefented; the former appearing for the moft part with the palms of their hands turned to the pofition that the backs generally occupy; and amid the vagaries of the latter are diftant garden walls and efpaliers infifting upon taking precedence of the mantlepieces and cabinets within the apartment, which, to a gentleman like Mr. Towle, devoting his energies to writing upon good manners, humility, and doing everything "*Genteel!*" muft have been particularly harrowing and diftreffing; fo that one cannot greatly wonder at the favage revenge he takes. But hear it in his own words, for

"None but himfelf can be his parallel."

One may almoft fancy that one fees him: his head thrown back, "quite genteel!" his eyes "in a fine frenzy rolling," his left hand on his hip, as with his right he prepared to make his fword leap from its fcabbard and fplit the unhappy *George Langly Smith*, of *Little Kirby Street, Hatton Garden, London*, as if he had been a Dunftable lark, predeftined to grilled bread crumbs and claret. But hufh! TOWLES LoQUITUR:

"The COPPER PLATES given in this Book coft *Seventeen Pounds, Six Shillings*, befides the expences of a *Law Suit*. . . . Engraved[1] by

---

[1] Query the lawfuit. The italics are Mr. Towles's, ftuck like larding-pins through and through the unhappy George Langly Smith.

George Langly Smith, in Little Kirby Street, Hatton Garden, London. The very great expence I have been at, I hope will atone and excuſe me from cenſure for publiſhing theſe Copper Plates: and I doubt not, but my Subſcribers will corroborate [!] *in their opinions with me*[!] that the following lines, taken from *Oldham*, are applicable to the above *Attempter* :—

' *To Mr. S. M——b.*

' Perhaps thou hop'dſt that thy obſcurity
Should be thy ſafeguard, and ſecure thee free.
No, wretch! *I* mean from thence to fetch thee out,
Like ſentenc'd felons to be dragg'd about;
Torn, mangled, and expos'd to ſcorn and ſhame,
I mean to hang and gibbet up THY NAME!' "

After this, doubtleſs exhauſted by the effort, exit TOWLE and enter ſubſcribers :—

" WE, whoſe names are hereunto Subſcribed, do approve the following Sheets, containing the firſt RUDIMENTS OF A POLITE EDUCATION, and recommend them, as very uſeful and proper to be introduced into all *Schools* and Families."

Here follows, not a ſingle name, but a long blank ſheet.

It is to be hoped, however, that the great TOWLE himſelf conſidered that by this ſtrict preſervation of the anonymous his ſubſcribers were behaving " very genteel," and that the large

white blank fpace left after their note of admiration was at once a delicate and a humorous
way of intimating to him, that inftead of a
vulgar, ordinary fubfcription, they gave him
carte blanche.

Then comes the preface ; but no, that is merely
folemn ftupidity turned up with bad grammar,
and therefore not worth tranfcribing ; but there
is a note appended to it, pointed out by a
typographical hand, that really *is* noteworthy !
Ecco !—

" The Author humbly hopes to find Favour,
in the judgment of his fuperiors, in Age and
Learning, and that they will view this Work as
a *Juvenile Attempt*, and pafs over in filence all
fuch Errors as may occur, unlefs of a Criminal
Nature." !

True it is indeed, that not *only* the evil but fometimes "the good men do ' lives' after them;" for
the foregoing would be an invaluable model note
(with perhaps another fort of note inclofed in it)
for every author to fend with his book to each
of the *Reviews.* If it could not infure a puff,
which depends more upon cliqueifm than even
money or merit, ftill it could not fail to ward
off a blow, except, perhaps, in the inftance of
The "S——y R——w," which, even in the teeth
of fo humble and touching an appeal, might be
capable of this fort of growl :—

" In compliance with the author's requeſt, we
paſs over his work in ſilence ; but muſt proteſt
againſt his having publiſhed it at all, as that
appears to us fully to come under the denomination of what he terms 'Errors of a Criminal
Nature.' "

As I have invited you, reader, to this *petit
diner fin*, I ſhall now proceed to recommend to
you ſome of the choice *morceaux* of the feaſt,
not, however, helping you too largely ; for *that*
Mr. Towle, in his valuable rules " How to
Behave *Genteel* at Meals," eſpecially depre-
cates in ſome ſarcaſtic (or, being at dinner, I
ſhould ſay, cutting) remarks upon one Mr. *Lombum*,
of whom he has informed poſterity that " though
he eats but little, that is no reaſon he ſhould
pick and cull the meat, and take juſt what he
thinks proper. If any pudding comes to table
you ſee he cuts it half, and eats not one fourth
part of what he cuts.[1] So ſome of the company
go without any, unleſs they will accept of his
plate[!] If a fowl comes to table he takes the

---

[1] A very good plan of Mr. Lombum's for preventing the
" company " coming again, and an evident proof that in
claſſic Oxford in thoſe days they imitated the noble frugality
of the ancients, when not ſacrificing at a great banquet, and
might, like Seneca, have been ſurpriſed with a ſolitary meſs of
lentil pottage, or, like Pliny the Younger, over a ſingle gentleman of a grey mullet and a cucumber.

prime pieces,[1] though he eats but little of them
either. In fhort, he ferves everything fo that
comes in his way. If a tart comes to table he
cuts it, though nobody eats it,[2] and at the fame
time he will put in the fpoon, take out the juice,
and eat it with the fame fpoon, and after it has
been in his mouth[!] he will put it into the tart
again, for the perfons at table to help themfelves
to, if they pleafe!"[3]

A grain of example being at all times better
than a bufhel of precept, I fhall ftudioufly avoid
giving you too large pieces of Mr. Towle's pudding (which I am fure you would *Lumbumife* if
I did), and merely pick out the plums here and
there. But before he expatiates on manner and
deportment he has very properly two preliminary
articles, entitled "OUR DUTY TO GOD AT HOME,"
and "OUR DUTY TO GOD OUT WALKING"!

In the firft of which he tells us (and *this* may
not be altogether new to the readers of the

---

[1] Which really *is* foul, and *not* fair.

[2] If nobody eat it? Why, oh Magnus Towle! be fo fevere
upon the taking ways of MR. LUMBUM? for by this it would
appear that they *all* cut the tart.

[3] I knew it! There is always an adequate reafon for everything, however ftrange or unwonted, if people could only find
it out, and this fpoony behaviour of MR. LUMBUM's fully
accounts for the reft of "the company" exercifing their felf-
denial with regard to the tart.

present generation), that it is our duty to God at home *to say our prayers!* but that "out of doors this is not necessary, as our duty there *is to be-have genteel!*"[1]

*   *   *   *   *

But "Chapter XII. *Of Behaviour in Walking with Company*," though rather a long walk, is so very amusing, that it cannot possibly fatigue anybody.

"The next thing necessary," says Mr. Towle, "is to know how to behave in walking with company abroad.

"In the first place, consider who you are walking with and their RANK (with a big R !) and in how great a degree they are your supe-riors, or whether they are your equals. If they are your superiors in age, fortune, or birth, to them respect is due. By such considerations you

---

[1] It is quite clear from this that the terse TOWLE, evidently in advance of his age as he was, had no suspicion of open-air preaching then "looming in the future," or he would have ventilated the subject in his own inimitable manner; for in another part of his valuable work he tells us that our prayers in church are *not* acceptable to the Almighty "*unless we behave ourselves genteel*"! which he explains by warning the ladies against ogling through the sticks of their fans, and the men "doing *the like* over the rims of their hats," and "*both not omitting to bow or curtsey, polite and genteel, to their Supe-riors in the pew, every time they rise from kneeling at their devotions.*"

will always know how to addreſs and behave politely to the Company you are with. It is impoſſible that you ſhould behave well or *genteel*, and in a proper manner, unleſs you always take a full view of them firſt near[1] and attentive, then you will be able to behave to every one according to their Rank. Should you ſuffer yourſelf to neglect this rule, you will daily give offence undeſignedly, and by that means bring yourſelf to Diſgrace. It will alſo render you an improper perſon for private Company as alſo public. A man muſt ſhine in private Company, even to appear in a decent manner in public.[2]

" I hope you will obſerve what I have ſaid, and then it will anſwer our purpoſe. As I have given you to underſtand that it is neceſſary for you to know your Company,[3] I ſhall ſay no more of it, but proceed. If you are walking with your ſuperiors, pay the reſpect due to them, then will you give ſatisfaction.[4] It is your duty to give

---

[1] This really is making no allowance whatever for the many perſons, as well as things, to whom
" Diſtance lends enchantment to the view."

[2] Towle! Towle! *nous avons changé tout cela.*

[3] Mr. Towle is here evidently labouring under a ſort of vulgar curioſity to know and find out who you are, employing for that purpoſe the ingredients of the proverbial receipt, "Tell me your company and I'll tell you what you are."

[4] Here the author had evidently a retroſpective eye to footmen.

them the wall in walking and to walk even with
them, if there is not too great a number to walk
abreaft [!] In this cafe you fhould agree to make
two parties; then take care to let your elders
walk firft; it is their place, therefore never attempt
to take it of them, becaufe that would be behaving rude and ungenteel [!]; but when you are
walking with your father or mother, governefs
or teachers, then it is your place to go firft, and
take care you walk upright and genteel.[!] In
the next place you are to walk at a proper
diftance, not too nigh nor too far off; the inconveniencies arifing from walking too nigh or too
far off are difagreeable to them that walk firft,
viz. if they are ladies you may in all probability
tread upon their GOWNS, SAQUES, or TROL-
LOPEES [!], and very often may by an unguarded
ftep tread upon their heels; this would not be
very acceptable to the ladies. Should it be dark
and dirty,[1] you would by going too nigh fplafh
them all over; this they will think rude of you,
although it might happen to any one in the dark.
The only way to avoid thefe inconveniencies is

---

[1] In this counfel Mr. Towle (who appears to have been a
perfon of fuch fubtle, fatirical wit as to make it almoft baffle
detection,) muft have meant a fling at the Mohawks, who *were*
addicted to walking in large parties abreaft in the dark and in
the dirt, otherwife among no clafs were thefe miry tenebrious
perambulations among the " Games and Paftimes of England."

not to walk too nigh them; about two yards is a proper diftance; on the other hand you are not to exceed that fpace, if you do you are guilty of bad manners to a great degree for walking fix or ten yards behind your company, or as though you were talking of them or upon fome fubject that would be improper for them to hear, or as if you would rather walk by yourfelf. In the next place, it would be inconvenient to them to make you hear when they thought proper to fpeak to you, which is very often the cafe, as you and every one muft think. Be always attentive to what they fay, and walk quietly and decently; avoid all coxcombical airs in walking, for this[1] *will give every one that fees you an opportunity of knowing that you are a fool full as well as if they had been long acquainted with you.*[!] But I hope by this time you are fo well acquainted with the rules of behaviour as to require my faying no more on felf-love and felf-conceit, fo I will pro-

---

[1] Surely Towle the Terpfichorean does not, in his impenetrably difguifed irony, mean to fay that by *not* giving himfelf coxcombical airs the mythological fample young gentleman here invidioufly pointed out would be anticipating the "courfe of time" by the revelation alluded to in the italicifed paffage that follows. No, no; it muft only be one of thofe grammatical errors into which he is conftantly falling, in his laudable anxiety to avoid "criminal" ones, and he muft have inadvertently fubftituted "this" for they, and fo have achieved a *non*-fenfe.

ceed in my difcourfe. Let all your converfation that paffes be fpoken in a foft tone of voice, in fuch a manner as your company may hear, but you are not obliged to fpeak fo loud that all the people in the ftreet may hear too ; there is not any thing that points out low, ill bred perfons more than talking loud in the ftreet. [True, this, at all events.] If you fuffer yourfelf to con-verfe in that manner, fhould you be worth ten millions of money [!] you would be only one degree above any one in Billingfgate.[1] It is not money that makes the gentleman[2] always. Money does, I own, with fome bafe people ; but what are they better than beafts of the field ? No, not one jot ; they even wrong their God of his due ; then how can men expect to meet with civility and love from thofe who even make

---

[1] It might have been fo in *your* time, Towle, but other times other Towles, alias tactics, and *we* are wifer in our generation ; for any one with even a tithe of that " *very genteel*," becaufe by no means common, competency, TEN MILLIONS ! may not only talk as loud, but be as low as he pleafes. For this is really the Golden Age, or at leaft the age of gold. We read of ponies being fhod with golden fhoes in Auftralia, but there is nothing original in this ; for a certain potentate of the Netherlands, not fit to " mention to ears polite," has always had *his* hoofs fhod with gold when he wifhed to make fure of a good footing amongft us.

[2] Another error this in the Towlean philofophy, for the gentleman who makes money makes all other gentlemen bow down to him—or to his money, which is all the fame thing.

no fcruple to wrong their juft God for that falfe and bafe god, MONEY, and make a wrong ufe of it for it ever? Obferve thefe words:—
'It is eafier for a camel to go through the eye of a needle than for a rich man to enter into the kingdom of heaven.' Notwithftanding they have fuch a caution from the mouth of the Son of God, I may venture to fay [indeed, Towle, you may!] that there are fome people who make money their god, and none other do they worfhip. They are fworn enemies to humanity and to the poor, they even hate all kind of civility and politenefs, except what is fhewn to themfelves; that man is a fine gentleman who has money; they never inquire how he got it, or whom he wronged; what orphan or what widow; or whom he plundered or murdered; all wrongs are looked on as a perfection in him. The money makes the gentleman with fome perfons, but I hope it never will with you, for men who are fo inclined will even forfeit their own fouls, they will fell their daughters, in fhort, they will ftick at nothing to get money, and yet they can only have the. ufe of it for this life." [1]

     *   *   *   *   *

---

[1] Few perfons are fo *exigeant* as to require, or fo unreafonable as to expect, it longer. It is doubtful (mind, I do not venture to fay that it is *certain* he would not,) yes, it *is*

Mr. Towle then continues for four pages more in the same strain, but as it is also nearly *verbatim* the same as what I have just helped you to, allow me to recommend to you a few of his other *friandises.*

ARTICLE II. : or SECOND COURSE.

" When your company think proper to go into a house, church, or *any other place*,[1] you must let *them* go first; should it be *an* house where you are not acquainted then you are to stay till you are asked to walk in, which you

---

doubtful whether even the Marquis of ———— contemplates having his rental, his cheque-book, and the key of the cellar packed up in his coffin with him. But *quand même, cui bono?*

[1] Could Mr. Towle, by the stress he lays on "*any other place*," have been alluding to the story of a certain testy old gentleman who upon one occasion, when about to take his diurnal drive, on being asked by the coachman, " Where to, sir ?" responded in his gruffest tones, " To the D—l." The obedient Jehu made no reply, but gathered up his reins and proceeded. Several hours elapsed under the usual slow jog-trot family-coach pace, during which the old gentleman's choler decreased as his hunger increased, so, pulling the check, he cried out, " Where on earth are you going, John ?" " Where you told me, sir," was the reply. John's master, being tickled at once by the fun and the phlegmatic philosophy of this answer, said, with a latent twinkle in his eye and an expression of bland remonstrance on his lip, " Well, but how will you manage about yourself when you get there ?" " Oh, no need to trouble about *me*, sir. *I shall back you in.*"

may depend upon it they *will do*. [Query, " You will be."] When you *are* aſked to walk in, take off your hat in your left hand, bow, and go in ; if they aſk you to ſit down, do it, and at the ſame time bow or curtſey, ſaying, ' Thank you, ſir,' or ' madam.' Take your ſeat at THE BOTTOM OF THE ROOM, if you have not a place told you to ſit in ; ſhould the room not be full of company then you are to take the bottomeſt ſeat next your company ; but you will have a chair placed for you to ſit in, or at leaſt there ought to be one. You muſt be cautious here in your behaviour, never to ſpeak unleſs you are ſpoken to, then addreſs them Sir or Madam, as I have given you inſtructions before how to addreſs every one, according to their quality and fortune.

" Always be conciſe in your opinion, expreſs your ſentiments in few words, and as diſtinct as poſſible. [Very good advice.] When your company think proper to go let your ſuperiors go out firſt ; then take leave of the company that are in the room in a genteel manner, paying a juſt reſpect to them all. When you come to the ſtreet door bow to the gentleman or lady that waits on you to the door ; *for you may depend on't they are very genteel people who wait on their gueſts to the door.* I would not have you miſunderſtand me wrong, and think that I mean they are rich, and the like.[1] No; I mean that they know how to behave polite and genteel. If they come to the door, bow with all the respect you are master of, saying, 'Madam,' or 'Sir, I am very sorry to give you this trouble.' And again, should there be no servant to open the door, if you are well acquainted with the house, sooner than give the master or mistress the trouble to open the door, say, in a polite manner, 'Madam,' or 'Sir, give me leave to open the door, we can do very well without giving you the trouble to attend us to the door;' but if they insist on it do not dispute with them, but take care not to detain them at the door, least they catch cold thereby.

"Now you are in the streets again, if you see anything that may appear surprising do not stop to look at it, but look at it as you go on; should you stop, as I have said before, it would be rude, but I shall forbear to say more, as I have said enough before.[2] You are never to call after any of your acquaintance in the public street, but if you see any one that you want to speak to go up

---

[1] Every one knows there is *nothing* like being rich, therefore what *can* "rich and the *like*" possibly mean? Perhaps some of our modern writers who affect those most detestable of all vulgarisms of the 15th, 16th, 17th, and 18th centuries, "the like," and "such like," may be able to tell, but I really cannot.

[2] I think so too.

to him firſt.[1] It is not genteel, neither is it
polite, to point[2] at any one, or to point in at
any ſhop window. Should you ſee any thing
pleaſing to the company and would communicate
it, ſpeak decently thus: 'Gentlemen,' or 'Ladies,
if you pleaſe to look this way here is ſomething
that will pleaſe you;' but forbear to ſay 'Look
yonder,' or 'Look there,' for if you *was* to expreſs
yourſelf ſo it would be imitating oyſter girls or
boys; for none but thoſe ſort of people uſe ſuch
kind of language. In the next place, you are to
avoid dreſſing yourſelf in the ſtreet.[3] Poſſibly
you may aſk what I mean by *that?* But to ſave
you the trouble of aſking I will do my endeavours
to inform you. In the firſt place, I mean that
I would have you appear decent as you walk
along, free from affectation, pride, *and the like.*
But in order that you may underſtand me better
I will give you an example, by ſhewing you that
inſufferable Fop, Mr. GAUDY. This is a fop,
of whom I will do my endeavours to draw the
outlines, as near as poſſible, but it would be a work

---

[1] This is generally conſidered to be a neceſſary preliminary.
[2] Of courſe, this does not apply to pointers with regard to
partridges; therefore it is to be hoped, even if not "genteel,"
they will be too well bred to conſider this remark perſonal.
[3] A bedroom cannot be too airy, but certainly ſuch an
al freſco dreſſing-room as the ſtreet would be anything but
deſirable, to ſay nothing of the impropriety of ſuch a proceed-

of time to draw a juft PIECE of him,[1] but I think
you will have an opportunity of feeing him if
you will walk this way. O, now you fee him,
there he is! now you will fee fifty different motions
betwixt here and the bottom of the ftreet; now
you fee him beholding himfelf! now he looks
behind him, to fee who is looking at him; every
one that looks at him he thinks admires him;[2]
if a lady looks at him he imagines fhe admires
him as fomething more than flefh and blood and
real nature. There! obferve him rubbing his hands,
beholding them with admiration. Now you fee
he fmiles with the pleafing thoughts that his hands
begin to make him amends for all the trouble and
expenfe he has been at *about his hands!* Ah,
what makes you look at me fo? what do you
wonder at? you will fay, For heaven's fake, what
expenfe can he have been at about his hands?

---

ing. But this, perhaps, is what is meant in the old plays of
the Congreve and Wycherly fchool, by having " the *airs* of a
man, or woman, of *quality.*" *Now* the only airs of a ftreet
are thofe ground on a barrel organ.

[1] Now really, unartiftic ignoramufes might have fuppofed
that it was eafier to draw a *piece* of Mr. GAUDY than even the
outline, though, as a whole, he might have required all the
vermilion and gamboge lavifhed on his funfets and funrifes
by the late Mr. Turner, R.A.

[2] This diftemper, oh Towle! I can affure you, is quite as
much an epidemic among " gents " in pegtops in our day as it
was among Gaudys in periwigs in yours.

Why, I will tell you, thefe kind of people lie in
lamb-fkin gloves,[1] and go to a great expenfe in
buying waters to wafh their hands in to make
them look fair. But obferve him pulling down
his fhirt-fleeves;[2] now placing his ruffles, there,
now his neckcloth, now his hat. But obferve
that porter who comes along; it is ten to one
that he hits that thing on his fhoulder againft
him, for you fee he looks likely enough to do it,
for he pays no refpect to perfons. Ah! ah! now
you fee, juft I faid, fo it is; you fee he has *dif-
obliged* [!] Mr. Gaudy's hair, which was fo curioufly
dreffed, and fplafhed the dirt all over him too.
That is very monftrous indeed, and you fee the
rogue fmiles, as if he had done it for the joke's
fake. Poor fop, quite out of patience, you fee;
he takes his handkerchief to wipe his ftockings,
and by hanging down his hands makes them red;
what a pity indeed to have his hands fo much
changed, *all along with fuch a fellow!* Notwithftanding this misfortune, you fee he is eaten up
with affectation; now his fhirt is not right, now
he is placing his neckcloth, now his finger is in
his hair, now he looks behind him, now his coat-
fleeves are pulled down, they are not low enough,

---

[1] Verily, this is only a venial offence, feeing that fome
perfons will lie in anything and through everything.

[2] Surely, oh Towle the Terrible! you would not have him
pull them up?

and if you were to follow him all day he would never be rightly dressed. Observe the first operator's shop for the hair, if he does not go in there; there, now he goes into the shop. Poor creature! you see he is quite sick, his face shows he is ready to faint with vexation. Now we will leave him there, to undergo a fatigue for an hour and a half."

Grateful in the extreme to Mr. Gaudy for having gone into the hairdresser's shop (though I don't exactly see how *that* was to get the mud off his stockings), I will now proceed, dear reader, to place before you the last of this feast of fragments, in the form of a panegyric and a philippic, by the masterly hand of Towle. The former you may consider as a *soufflé*, winding up our repast, and the latter as ginger ice, it is at once so cool and yet so spicy.

" MASTER LOUTES.

" A PANEGYRIC.

" Compliance is an honourable disposition of the mind [!] where it is truly united in *an* humane heart. Happy is that man who hath it in his possession; he is sure to be respected and esteemed in company; he condescends to oblige others in never contradicting their desires, if honourable and consistent with reason.

" This sort of complaisance makes him agreeable.[1] He is loved, because he is of an easy, flexible temper : his will seems not his own. Every desire of his friends would he do, and all that was in his power, in order that they might be happy. Master Loutes is of this complaisant turn. You cannot look at what you want[2] before he is up and fetches it, before you have time to ask. He doth it with so much good nature and ease, that you would imagine he was upon some peculiar business of his own, and all the time he is entirely studying what may please you. So sweet is the disposition of Master Loutes, there is not one day passes but he distinguishes himself by his complaisance and sweet temper."

> Once on a time lived Anacharsis Cloots,[3]
>   Who about the human race did howl ;
> But more than blest, thrice happy, Master Loutes,
>   You—you have found an orator in Towle !

---

[1] There cannot be a doubt of it.

[2] Then Mr. Loutes *père* must have been greatly to be pitied, as it is evident from this that Master Loutes was *up to everything*.

[3] Pronounced Clouts.

An Invidious Philippic,
not against Mother Church, but against Mothers at Church.

"'My little ladies, I will here give you friendly advice. I hope you will not take it amifs, as I think it my duty fo to do in everything that lies in my power.

"'When you are feated in your place at Church do not get up again till the fervice is begun; then rife, place your eyes on your prayer-book, and there keep them till fuch time as that part of the fervice is over. If you, on the contrary, get up and look about you, or through your fan at any one, you will be guilty of a breach of that modefty which is peculiar to your fex, or ought to be.'

"S. 'Yes, fir, I do not difpute your judgment, but I have feen my mamma and Lady *Mears* do fo.'

"M. 'Something extraordinary might happen. Very poffibly your mamma could not fee for the fun, that might be the caufe of it; and Lady *Mears* is always laughing, fhe being fenfible of the crime, though fhe has not prudence enough to avoid it; therefore fhe is afhamed to fhow her face.'

"S. 'Yes, fir, my mamma hath done it, that

fhe might look at L——y G——d's filk gown.
She hath bid me do fo too. She bought me and
herfelf a fan each, with holes in the mounts on
purpofe. She can tell all or moft of all the
ladies' dreffes that are in church. There is not a
ftranger but what fhe knows who they are with,
and what they had on, and who fuch and fuch
gentlemen looked at.'

" M. 'But my little lady, you may be miftaken.
This notice fhe may take when the fervice is
over.'

"S. 'No, fir, my mamma bid me obferve laft
Sunday, in the middle of the fermon, the parfon's diamond ring and his white hand.'

" M. 'Mifs, I will allow that you might underftand your mamma as fuch, but I'm inclined
to think that you are under a miftake. She
might tell you to mind the parfon and not play
with your hand and ring, for I am of an opinion
your mamma is of a more fedate turn, or ought
to be, after being the mother of ten children,¹ fo

---

¹ In claffing the prolific among the fedatives, does Mr.
Towle mean to imply that ten children are a fort of ma-
ternal henbane? But mark the mingled prudence and fine
irony of this paffage: " I am of *an* opinion that your mamma
is of a more fedate turn, *or ought to be!*" Then the fubtle,
Bellerephon plan he adopts for letting the mothers know what
their tell-tale daughters fay of them, by the way in which he
begs the queftion in thefe dialogues.

I hope you are under a miſtake; but my dear child, do not think I doubt your veracity, only you might miſtake the thing.' "

There are about twenty pages more, all in the ſame ſtrain—a fine and perfectly parliamentary one: in which he denounces all the impious horrors of the mamma's ogling propenſities in church, and then ſuddenly pulls up to tell " the little lady " that not for a moment does *he* ſuppoſe *her* mamma capable of anything of the kind.

But the moſt charming part of this truly charming work is Mr. Towle's modeſty, in what he himſelf would call " taking the bottomeſt place " [!] in the different eulogiums ſcattered throughout it; for it will be remembered that he was a dancing-maſter, and although, after ſetting forth all the gliding graces of the minuet, he ex-patiates eloquently on thoſe leſs dignified but more inſpiriting French dances, the *Rigadoon*, the *Louvre*, the *Courant*, and the *Borée*, and animadverts upon ladies' dreſſes, not ſparing their *ſacques*, *night-gowns*,[1] and *trollopees*, telling them

---

[1] At that time, what we call evening dreſſes were always called *night-gowns*, as they were in Elizabeth's time, when men's dreſſing-gowns were alſo called *night-gowns*; hence the following entry by her Majeſty's " privy purſe:" " To a fine Murray *Velut*, frizzed on the wrong ſide, choſe by her Highneſs as a night-gown for my Lord of Leiceſter."

how they are attired, or at leaft *how they ought to be !* (that favourite claufe of his), and finds ruffles " marvellous proper" things for grown-up ladies, but abominations for " little miffes,"— thereby, I fuppofe, meaning to fay, that young ladies fhould never be ruffled. Still, he never fays one word in praife of the charming art of which he is a profeffor till the very climax of his exhortations, when to be fure, to make up for loft time, he *does* " come it rather ftrong " by breaking out into the following exclamation, for which he has not even the kindnefs to prepare his readers, as we were once prepared for and warned againft the French invafion :—

" I believe it is beyond a doubt that dancing is acceptable to God ; and as a *proof* obferve thefe words—' *Praife Him in the cymbals and dances.*'"

And not another word does he add to this ftartling announcement. How could he, without making an anti-climax ?

But foon after, both in rhyme and reafon, he gives fome very good advice to the fairer part of the creation, as to their choice of colours ;

> One would think it was Minerva's owl
> Blandly preaching through the lips of Towle.

" There are different colours," faith he, as fome gentlemen among the Latin poets have faid before him, "that agree with different complexions, and this is a matter really worth the ladies' obfervation ; but this fubject I will leave to the ladies' own infpection," [query, felection ?] " only giving them the opinion of a poet that now lies before me."

Of *courfe*, as it is an underftood thing that poets excel in fiction, the poet *lies* before him.

> " Let the fair nymph in whofe plump cheeks are feen
> A conftant blufh, be clad in verdant green ; [1]
> In fuch a drefs the fportive fea-nymphs go,
> So in their graffy beds frefh rofes blow.
>
> " The lafs whofe fkin is like the hazel brown,
> With b ighter yellow fhould o'ercome her own ;
> But the fair maid in whofe pale cheeks of fnow
> No blufhes rife nor blooming rofes glow
>
> " Far above all fhould potent fcarlet fly,
> And fooner chufe the fable's mournful dye : [2]
> So the pale moon ftill fhines with pureft light,
> Cloath'd in the dufky mantle of the night."

One more *bonne-bouche*, and then Magnus Towle may be removed.

" The drefs is the next thing to be confidered.

---

[1] " Blue or yellow, or light green, *blue yellow* (again) ftraw, or ftriped filks of the fame colours."—TOWLE.

[2] " Or Pompadour." Strange advice, Mr. Towle, as Pompadour is orange ; certainly *not* a becoming tint to perfons of a pale complexion.

Every young lady ought to be dreſſed genteel; that is, in ſilk or linen, with linen according to it ; [?] the ſtockings ſilk or cotton, the ſhoes ſilk, or morocco, or ſtuff, neatly made ; for the feet are more the objeƈt of notice in *dancing* than any other part in *dancing*.

" Each young lady ought to be dreſſed according to her age. Whatever ladies wear ought to fit them,[1] for not anything is a greater diſadvantage than clothes badly fitted. Some mammas take a pleaſure in ſeeing the ſhoulders of their children left bare, even down to the elbows, but I promiſe them that there are many ill conſequences attending it ; but perhaps they will ſay it is looſe and genteel. Looſe, indeed, it is, and indecently genteel too. On the other hand, they may plead for an excuſe that they do not love to ſee their children confined about the ſhoulders, and that it gives them room to grow. *That* is my opinion too, even till their ſhoulders touch their ears, and *learns* them to grow ſluttiſh and ungenteel. I would recommend to thoſe who would have their children appear decent and genteel, to take care that their children's ſlips fit very exaƈtly on the ſhoulders, for it is of infinite ſervice to thoſe who are inclinable to

---

[1] Though this is true, yet it does not apply to truth, ſince *ex nihilo nihil* fit.

grow high-shouldered—it helps to keep their
shoulders down in their proper place. I shall
further recommend gathered tuckers as a decent
and absolutely necessary part of dress; it also
adds to a genteel fall[1] from the shoulders. Some
ladies may say : 'Oh sir! my daughter must appear agreeable, so fine a skin as she's got.' Ladies,
I agree with you ; a fine skin is agreeable, but
decency is much more so, especially if it add
beauty to the wearer.

"Hats, tippets, and shades [?] are not to be
worn in dancing ; *it is* [!] impertinent, awkward,
and clownish.   The dress of the neck I leave
every one to dress as they think proper (only
those who have long necks I advise them to wear
something, as that is genteel.)

"The next thing that demands our attention
is, the dress of the head. For young ladies
from three to fourteen years old, a feather, a
flower, egret, or *ribbond*, or pompoon; these
are proper for dancing in. Ladies above this
age may do as they please,[2] only I think the

---

[1] Query: Would Mr. Towle have considered the Falls of
Niagara as genteel, or too much of a fall, so as to come under
the category of the foregone philippic ?

[2] I rather think that *that* age, viz., when ladies may do as
they please, has not yet arrived, or even set out ; for though
"a good time" has long been announced as "coming" for

prefent fafhion is very becoming,—I mean the rolls, &c."[1]

Now we will go upftairs to coffee; and I hope, reader, you will think that " Le véritable Amphitryon eft celui chez qui l'on—danfe!"

the "boys," there has not been a word faid about any fuch "welcome gueft" being *en route* for the girls.

[1] Mr. Towle does not fpecify *what* rolls, but of courfe he means *French rolls*.

ON THE COMPARATIVENESS OF GREATNESS.

WE read in the old Chronicles, that "In the firſt of Queen Mary, the braveſt ſhip in England, called 'The Great Harry' (by reaſon of its having been built in Henry VIII.'s time, and called after him), was burnt through negligence at Woolwich. It was 1,000 tons; and the people did think that the ſudden deſtruction which had overtaken it [!] was a judgment of God's diſpleaſure at man's preſumption to build ſo mighty a veſſel, to try and maſter as it were His winds and waves, which can only be maſtered by Himſelf."

The logic of this is rather Hibernian; for once granted that we may, do, and have launched hazel-nut and walnut ſhells on God's great ocean, there can ſurely be no additional ſin in increaſing the ſize of theſe nut-ſhell crafts to

that of cocoa-nuts, or even of calabaſhes. We
ſmile at theſe little homœopathic and opaque
ſuperſtitions of our forefathers, and yet in this
our boaſted nineteenth century, when we have
achieved a more rare wonder than Mr. Rarey,
by taming the lightning to drive in our MAIL
PHAETONS, and when, if we have not actually
" put a girdle round the earth in forty minutes,"
we *have* thrown a chain acroſs the Atlantic,
ſtill, we have *not* outgrown, we have only changed
the *venue* of our ſuperſtition ; for when the
" Great Eaſtern " exceeded the " Great Harry "
by 22,600 tons,[1] it was not its coloſſal ſize that
alarmed the pious ſuſceptibilities of the " Britiſh

---

[1] The burden of the "Great Eaſtern" is 23,600 tons!
But the mighty "Great Eaſtern " itſelf pales (in all but ſize)
before the *liburnæ* of Caligula, of which Suetonius gives
ſuch a glowing deſcription ; thoſe fairy-tale like barks, made
of the perfumed cedar, with their party-coloured ſilken ſails,
ſilver cordage, purple and gilded ivory prows, their porticoes,
ſaloons, and baths, their fragrant and blooming gardens, luxuriant vines and variety of fruit-trees, in which triumphs of
art over nature the luxurious monſter, the to " laſcivious
tunings" of golden lutes, would loll the ſultry hours away, as
he ſkirted the ceſtus ſhores of lovely Campania.   Theſe
liburnæ, moreover, appear to have been a ſort of ſteamboats
with the ſteam left out, for they were impelled by three
wheels on each ſide, but without touching the water, conſiſt-
ing of eight ſpokes jutting out from the wheel about a hand's
breadth, and ſix oxen within, which, by turning an engine,
worked the wheels, the revolutions of which, driving the

Public," as a preſumptuous braving of Omnipotence, but ſimply its original name of the
"*Leviathan*"!!! which, why or wherefore folly
only knows (for it would indeed be a metaphy-
ſical puzzle to try and trace the origin of ſuch
an aſſociation of ideas), but certain it is, that in
the eſtimation of theſe worthies the name being
ſelected from the Bible, with a ſtrange inverſe holi-
neſs (?) on that account they ſeemed to conſider
profane, though no doubt, had it been chriſtened
the "Crocodile" they would not have winced a
letter; and yet Fry conſiders that the whole de-
ſcriptions of the "behemoth," "leviathan," and
"crocodile," in Job, all tally ſo remarkably in
every particular and peculiarity, as to be ſuppoſed
to mean one and the ſame monſter; and "behemoth," at ch. xl. ver. 19, is ſpoken of as "unequalled," and "leviathan" at ch. xli. ver. 33,
is alſo ſpoken of as unequalled, which cannot be
ſaid of either of two different animals or of two
diſtinct magnitudes; and moreover, the deſcription of the habits of the crocodile, given by all
naturaliſts and travellers, exactly agrees with
thoſe imputed to the "leviathan" or "behemoth" by Job. But as I ſaid before, ALL

water backward, impelled theſe *liburnæ* forward with ſuch
force and ſpeed that no three-oared galley was able either to
keep up with or to reſiſt them.

greatneſs, whether moral, phyſical, intellectual,
or ſocial, that of fame or that of conventionality
or chance, is wholly and ſolely Comparative, not
to ſay geographical, and the POSITIVE has, it is
to be feared, very little to do with its appre-
ciation among them. Further, I contend that
time and place are great make-weights, and that
the local has much to do with the laudatory.
"GREAT" was "Diana of the Epheſians," on
earth; ſhe ſhone rather leſs as Luna in the
celeſtial regions; dwindled into an "unprotected
female" as Proſerpine, in the infernal ones; became poſitively obnoxious as Hecate; and if,
under the travelling title of Trivia, ſhe had
occaſionally at ſome ſlippery croſs-road a dog, a
lamb, or a little honey offered to her in the way
of propitiation by a few timorous wayfarers,
ſtill, that was but poor compenſation for her
former ſplendour.   However, ſhe always had
the advantage of her former divinity hanging
about her; unlike mere mortals under a reverſe
of fortune, for they, poor wretches, invariably go
to the dogs, inſtead of getting even a ſingle dog
brought to them.   Then as a check to all earthly
greatneſs (or as Mr. Towle would ſay, what at
leaſt *ought to ſuch*), comes DEATH! with his grim
gambols, playing at bowls with crowns, ſcep-
tres, wiſe heads and wicked ones, and after his
paſtime, banqueting alike on golden hearts that

never beat but to good and glorious motives, or on grovelling, narrow ones, that never glowed with even ONE generous impulſe.

Edward III., " the glorious conqueror," as he was called in his own day, and certainly one of the moſt popular of Engliſh kings, "fell," as the chroniclers tell us, "into his laſt ſickneſs at Richmond. When he was drawing on, his concubine, Alice Pierce, came, and took the rings from his fingers, leaving him gaſping for breath. And the officers of his court rifled him of what-ſoever they could. A prieſt, lamenting the king's miſery, that among all his ſervants had none to aſſiſt him in his laſt moments, exhorted him to repent and implore the mercy of God. The king had loſt his ſpeech, but at theſe words uttered his mind imperfectly, and made ſigns of contrition; but his voice failing him in pro-nouncing the name of Jeſus, he yielded up the ghoſt."

A little goodneſs, however humble, unknown, and inſignificant, at this laſt ſupreme hour, that *muſt* ſtrike for *all*, is worth a world-wide great-neſs, falſely ſo called. Had Edward III. been a better man, though a leſs great king, that is, had he eſchewed flatterers and avoided Alice Pierces "*and the like*," he might have died with his rings on his fingers and his pockets unſcathed by the rifle corps movement. And he ſhould have done fo; for the fpark of facred fire was there, had he but kindled inftead of fmothering it. Alas, poor human nature! what know we of MOST of all—the drofs through which our fpirit works its way, upward and onward, to its HOME? As in the chemiftry of common things, the moft heterogeneous rubbifh goes to fine wine, jelly, or coffee, and bring them ultimately to that tranflucent purity that conftitutes their perfection, may it not be the fame with ourfelves? or as Wordsworth finely expreffes it in thofe magnificent lines of his—

> " Duft as we are, the immortal fpirit grows
> Like harmony in mufic: there is a dark
> Infcrutable workmanfhip that reconciles
> Difcordant elements, makes them cling together
> In one fociety. How ftrange, that all
> The terrors, pains, and early miferies,
> Regrets, vexations, laffitudes, interfufed
> Within my mind, fhould e'er have borne a part,
> And that a needful part, in making up
> The calm exiftence that is mine, when I
> Am worthy of myfelf! Praife to the end." [1]

Among the *vulgar errors* Sir Thomas Browne has omitted to note, is that *very* vulgar one of fuppofing AMBITION to be a noble paffion; when, on the contrary, it is one of *the* moft

[1] " The Prelude and Growth of a Poet's Mind," an Autobiographical Poem, by William Wordsworth. Moxon.

vulgar of paſſions, from being the moſt ſelfiſh, mean, ſordid, unſcrupulous, and conſequently un-chivalrous, of all the paſſions; for truly, moſt ambitious men may be accurately ſummed up in Lowell's lines—

> " He had been noble, but ſome great deceit
> Had turn'd his better inſtinct to a vice;
> He ſtrove to think the world was all a cheat,
> That power and fame were cheap at any price;
> That the ſure way of being ſhortly great
> Was ever to play life's game with loaded dice:
> Since he had tried the honeſt plan, and found
> That vice and virtue differ'd but in ſound."

And all this terrible ſelf-ſacrifice of body and ſoul—for ſuch it *literally* is—to find *all* Vanitas Vanitatum, Omnia Vanitas!

UPON THE GREAT DIFFERENCE OF THE SAME CIRCUMSTANCES IN OUR OWN CASE AND THAT OF OTHERS,

WHICH ALWAYS HAS EXISTED, AND IT IS TO BE FEARED ALWAYS WILL EXIST.

Written juſt after the Diſaſter of Sedan.

" Meus mihi, ſuus cuique eſt carus."—PLAUTUS.

HOW ſtrange and unforeſeen are the revenges which "the whirligig of Time" brings about! and in moſt of them how inciſively Nemeſis points the moral! At the preſent criſis it is curiouſly intereſting, to read by the glare of the torch of diſcord of the preſent Franco-Germanic war, Voiture's letter of panegyric on Cardinal Richelieu a brace of centuries ago, upon *his* annexation of Alſace and Lorraine; *the* letter in fact which Monſieur Perrault compared to Pliny's panegyric upon Trajan. Well, compariſons are proverbially

odious, and sometimes even odorous, as Mrs. Mal-
aprop has it; but if the shade of Pliny retains a
shadow of the good sense he possessed in the
flesh it will only smile and glide on, remembering
that the comparison was made by a Frenchman.
But the letter itself contains such good advice to
victors as well as vanquished, that it is a thousand
pities that all Germany, as well as all France,
cannot spare time from the glorious work of
butchering each other, to " read, mark, learn, and
inwardly digest" it. *Cela posé*, I will give a trans-
lation of the letter *in extenso*:—

" I am not one of those, as you would seem to
imply, who delight to improve all my Lord Cardinal's actions into miracles and waft his praises
beyond due bounds, and who, while they would
make the world believe well of him, sacrifice all regard to credibility. On the other hand, I am not
of such a base detracting nature as to hate a man
merely because he is above the rest of the world,
neither will I suffer myself to be carried away by
popular prepossessions, which I know generally
speaking to be unjust. I consider him with an
unprejudiced judgment, where passion has nothing
to do on the one side or the other; and I behold
him with the same eyes that posterity will behold
him. And certainly *two hundred years hence*,[1] when

---

[1] M. Voiture did *not* foresee that Lorraine and Alsace

thofe who look upon him after us fhall read in
our hiftory that the great Cardinal de Richelieu
demolifhed Rochelle, confounded the heretics, and
by one fingle *coup de main* took thirty or forty of
their cities all at once—when they fhall come
to know, that at the time of his adminiftration
the Englifh were beaten and repulfed, Picardy
conquered, Caffel relieved, Lorraine annexed to
France, the greateft part of Alfatia fubjugated by
us, the Spaniards defeated at Vellaine and Avien;
I fay, that when they fhall find that *while he* pre-
fided over our affairs France had not one neigh-
bour over whom fhe did not gain fome important
victory or town, if they have the leaft drop of
French blood in their veins and any love for the
honour of their country, can they read thefe things
without having a great love for him? And do
you think they will love or efteem him the lefs
becaufe the payments of the Hôtel de Ville came
in fomewhat of the floweft? or becaufe fome new
offices were erected? Great things cannot be done
without great expenfe, and to cramp them for want
of money is to maim their execution. But if we
are to look upon a kingdom as immortal, and to
confider the advantages it will reap in future ages,
as if they were *actually prefent*, let us compute how

would be wrefted back from the great Cardinal's dead grafp
by a German Richelieu.

many millions this man, who they pretend has ruined France, has faved her by the bare taking of Rochelle? which town two thoufand years hence, in all the minorities of our kings, upon every dif-content of our nobles, and upon all occafions of revolt, would moft certainly have rebelled, and have entailed upon us a perpetual expenfe. Our kingdom had only two enemies to fear: the Hugue-nots and the Spaniards. My Lord Cardinal no fooner entered upon affairs but he immediately re-folved to ruin both? Was it poffible for him to form more glorious or more advantageous defigns? He has happily effected the one, but not com-pleted the other. However, if he has failed in his firft defign, thofe who now cry out that it was a rafh unreafonable refolution to pretend to attack and humble the power of Spain, and that experi-ence had fufficiently fhown it, yet would they not have been as forward to condemn his defign of ruining the Huguenots? Would they not have told us that we ought not to have embarked in an enterprife wherein three of our kings [Francis II., Charles IX., and Henry III.] had mifcarried, and which the late king [Henri Quatre] did not fo much as think of? And would they not have concluded, as erroneoufly as they do in this other affair, that the thing was not feafible merely becaufe it was not already done? But let us confider, I befeech you, if it was his or Fortune's fault, that he has not as yet accomplished the design. Let us see what method he took to effect it, and what engines he set in motion. Let us examine whether he has failed much in felling that mighty tree, the House of Austria, and has not shaken the very root of the trunk, whose two branches covered the north and the west, and overshadowed the rest of the earth. He went as far as the northern pole to find out that hero[1] who seemed predestined to lay the axe to it and bring it to the ground. It was his skill, combined with his thunder, which filled all Germany with fire and desolation, and the noise of which echoed through the world. But when this tempest was dispersed and Fate had turned away the impending blow, did *he* stop short in his course or cease his designs? and did he not bring the Empire lower than it had been brought by the losses of the battle of Leipsic and that of Lützen? His astuteness and energy raised us up suddenly an army of forty thousand men in the heart of Germany, with a general at the head of them who was master of all the great qualities requisite to bring about a revolution in any state. If the King of Sweden threw himself into danger more than became a person of his design and rank, and if the Duke of Friedland, by over-delaying his enterprise, suffered it to get wind and be discovered, was it possible for the

---

[1] Gustavus Adolphus.

Cardinal either to charm the bullet which killed
the former in the midſt of victory, or render the
latter impervious to the blows of a *partiſan*? And
if after this diſmal blow, to complete the ruin
of our affairs, the generals who commanded the
armies of our allies before Nördlingen gave battle
at an unſeaſonable time, was it poſſible for the
Cardinal, who was above two thouſand leagues
from the ſpot, to change this reſolution, and check
the unadviſable raſhneſs of thoſe who, for an empire that would have been the certain price of
victory, would not ſtay three days longer? Thus
you ſee it was impoſſible to ſave the Houſe of
Auſtria and hinder the execution of the Cardinal's
deſigns, which ſome perſons pretend were ſo raſh
that had not Fortune wrought three ſurpriſing
miracles, that is to ſay, three great events, which
in all probability it would have been thought never
could have happened—I mean the death of the
King of Sweden, that of the Duke of Friedland,
and the loſs of the battle of Nördlingen—you will
tell me he has no reaſon to complain of Fortune
for croſſing him in this, ſince ſhe had ſerved him
ſo faithfully in all his other deſigns; ſince ſhe put
places into his hands without his ſo much as laying
ſiege to them; and ſince alſo by her favour he
commanded armies ſo ſucceſsfully without the leaſt
experience to direct him, ſhe leading him always
as it were by the hand, and bringing him ſafe out

of the greateft perils into which he had thrown himfelf, and made him appear, bold, wife, and prefcient without any merit of his. Let us therefore behold him in his evil fortune, and examine if even then he evinced lefs boldnefs, wifdom, and forefight. Our affairs were in no very good pofture in Italy, and as it is the deftiny of France to win battles and lofe armies, ours was exceedingly diminifhed ever fince the laft victory we had gained over the Spaniards. We had not much better luck before Dôle, where the length of the fiege made us apprehend its ill fuccefs, when we received news that the enemy had entered Picardy, that they had at the firft onfet taken Caffel, Caftelet, and Corbie; and that thefe three places, which ought to have held out eight months, fcarcely held out as many days. All was in fire and afhes to the banks of the Oife; we might behold from our fuburbs the fmoke of the villages which the enemy had burnt. All the world was alarmed at this fudden progrefs, and the capital city of our kingdom was in the higheft confternation. In the midft of thefe calamities advices came from Burgundy that the fiege of Dôle was raifed, and from Xaintoigne that fifty thoufand peafants were up in arms, and that it was feared the infection would fpread to Poitou and Guienne. Ill news came pouring upon us from all parts, the whole face of heaven was overcaft, the tempeft invaded us from

every fide, and we had not the leaft profpect of
good fortune to fupport us in thefe extremities.
We could not perceive daylight through the
fmalleft aperture. But in all this darknefs did the
Cardinal fee lefs clearly than at other times? Did he
lofe either his judgment or refolution? And during
this ftorm, did he not always keep the rudder in
one hand and the compafs in the other? Did he call
out for the long-boat to fave himfelf? And if the
great veffel which he fteered was deftined to be
caft away, did he not fhow that he was the firft
man who refolved to perifh? Was it Fortune
that delivered him out of this labyrinth, or his
own prudence and magnanimity? Our enemies
were within fifteen leagues of Paris, and his were
in the town; he received daily advices that cabals
were held and defigns formed to ruin him; France
and Spain were, if I may fo exprefs myfelf, joined
in a confpiracy againft him alone. Now amidft
all thefe threatening circumftances and concur-
rences, in the midft of fo dreadful and black a
conjunction, how did this man look, whom they
pretended would be caft down upon the leaft ill
fuccefs, and who, as they gave out, had fortified
Havre de Grace on purpofe to make it a place of
retreat in cafe of any difafter? He does not go
one ftep backwards for all this. He is taken
up with the dangers of the ftate, and not with
his own; and all the alteration we could obferve

in him at this time was, that whereas he never used to go abroad without two hundred guards, he now walked out every day attended only by five or six gentlemen. All the world must own that an adversity supported with so good a grace and with so much courage is to be preferred to victory and prosperity itself. He did not appear to me so great and victorious, even when he made his entry into Rochelle, as then; and the daily visits he made to the arsenal were, in my opinion, more glorious to him than his famous expedition on the other side of the mountains, when he took Pignerol and Sufa. Therefore, let me conjure you to open your eyes and to prepare for beholding so bright an object. Lay aside your aversion to the man who is so happy in revenging himself upon his enemies, and cease to wish ill to him who knows how to turn it to his glory by bearing himself so undauntedly under it. Leave your party before they leave you, as a great number of the great Cardinal's enemies have done, who were converted by the last miracle they saw him perform. If the war should cease, as there is reason to hope it will, he'll soon find a way to gain the rest over to his side. Being so wise as he is, he must certainly know, after so much experience, what is best for us, and will aim all his designs so as to make us the most flourishing people in the world, after he has made us the most formidable.

"He will content himfelf with an ambition that is to be preferred before all others, and which is practifed but by few : I mean, to make himfelf the beft and moft beloved man in the kingdom, and not the greateft and moft feared. He knows that the nobleft and the moft lafting conquefts are thofe of the heart and the affections; that laurels are barren plants, which yield nothing but fhade, and are not to compare with the harveft and fruits with which PEACE is crowned. He confiders that it is *nothing near fo meritorious to enlarge the limits of a kingdom a hundred leagues and more as to leffen our taxes twelve pence in the pound ; and that there is lefs grandeur and real glory in defeating a hundred thoufand men than leaving twenty millions at their eafe and in fecurity.*

"Thus this mighty genius, who has been hitherto folely employed in contriving and raifing funds for the fupport of the war, in raifing recruits, taking cities, and gaining battles, will for the future wholly bufy himfelf in eftablifhing PEACE, WEALTH, and PLENTY. The fame head which brought forth a Pallas armed cap-a-pie, will fhow us the goddefs with her olive branch, peaceable, gentle, and learned, accompanied by all thofe arts which are generally to be found in her train. He will publifh no more new edicts but fuch as may tend to reftrain luxury and promote commerce. Thofe great veffels that were built to carry our arms beyond the Straits, fhall for the future only bear our merchants and keep the feas open, and we fhall have no more war but with the Algerines. Then the enemies of my Lord Cardinal will not be able to fpeak, as hitherto they have not been able to act, againft him. Then the citizens of Paris fhall be his guards, and he will be convinced how much more pleafing and fatisfactory it is to hear his praifes in the mouth of the people than in that of the poets. But I befeech you not to ftand aloof till this happens, and ftay not to be his Friend till you are forced to be fo ; but if you are refolved to perfift in your opinion I fhall not attempt to ufe any violence to diffuade you from it. However, be not fo unjuft as to take it ill that I have defended my own ; and I freely promife you to read whatever you may think fit to write to me by way of anfwer, when the Spaniards have taken Corbie.—I am, Sir, your moft obedient fervant, Voiture."

It is to be wifhed that not only thofe of France and Germany, but all the European Powers, would carefully read and ponder the italicifed paragraph in the foregoing letter. For civilization is a *fiafco*, and verbal Chriftianity an impious mockery, fo long as nations from time to time continue to get up monfter human fhambles, call

it "glory," inſtead of what it *is*—gory, and thank
Providence for the amount of wholeſale murder ;
as if they ignored that great myſterious faɗ, that
although, for ſome inſcrutable purpoſe, God *per-
mits* evil of every ſort, yet He never *endorſes* it,
even when it calls itſelf Viɗory. As for Napoleon
III., no one of courſe in this enlightened age, is ſo
ſilly as to defend a dead lion. Given a uſurper,
and of courſe you have that moſt ſelf-ſeeking
and unſcrupulous of all things — AMBITION.
Still, the hollow, bitter world, with all its unlimited ingratitude, ſhould not quite ſo ſoon forget, and ſtill leſs ſhould the French forget, the
two decades of plethoric proſperity, European
influence, and above all and more precious than
all, the *order*, he beſtowed upon France. As for,
at this time of day, colleɗing cairns from which
to lapidate the fallen Emperor's domeſtic im-
morality, *that* is ſuch a very pot-and-kettle proceeding for any one man to do to another, that
it is doubly contemptible, from being both hypo-
critical and ridiculous. The very worſt that can
be ſaid of the ex-Emperor—for it includes all that
is evil—is, that he graduated at GORE HOUSE
—that cradle of all vice, and tomb of all virtue.
It is to be hoped *that* emporium of ſocial, political, and literary turpitude, may never have a
ſucceſſor.

"Di talem terris avertite peſtem !"

AN ESSAY UPON ESSAYS.

IF there be fuch a thing as fincerity in authors or truth in books, effay writing is unqueftionably the trueft and moft fincere of any fpecies of compofition; for I take it that an effay is, as it were, the lining of at leaft one particular phafe of the writer's mind, and confequently a modified reflex of the entire tone and calibre of his whole nature. But, as in the planetary fyftem the fun is the original of the moon, fo are there in the fcheme of human intelligences folar minds, felf-radiating in their own ftupendous, inexhauftible, creative, and vivifying powers, and lunar minds, which reflect their rays, with great beauty and clearnefs, it is true, and with a certain influence upon the flux and reflux of events which form the tides of human opinions, but with no *univer-fality* of power to penetrate into the moft fecret receffes of the innermoft core of the great and many-pulfed heart of nature, like the omnipresent original luminary. For the fire, the sacred fire, is the *soul* and centre of the one, and its mere calm, cold, simulated reflex is the intellectual head-work of the other. Among these rare solar minds were those of Shakespeare and Montaigne; the Universal was *in*, and emanated *from* both; while pre-eminent among the pale, cold, reflective, intellectual luminaries, were Lords Bacon and Shaftesbury. They might have written, but I doubt if either of them would have ever taken up the trade of THINKERS (for such it was with them), if Montaigne had not left them such an inexhaustible mine of original ore to work, and such ready excavated ingots to stamp into popular currency. But here comes the great difference between the original luminary, with its glowing soul, that by one electric spark carries yours on, and up, into the illimitable worlds of thought, and those mere cold, soulless, reflected, intellectual lights, which indeed shed a beauty and a charm upon even the most ordinary and commonplace things, and show us clearly all that is to be seen in the physical world, making a sort of moral inventory for us of the property our mother Nature has bequeathed to us, and marking off those particular items that our stepmother Fate will try to defraud us out of, but which from themselves, possessing no vital warmth, cannot impart it, and from whose

catalogue of dry, hard, incontrovertible, unpro-
ductive, if not unsuggestive facts, we derive about
as much pleasure and *real* good as we do when
Suetonius informs posterity that Tiberius Cæsar's
eyes were so luminous that he could see every
object in the dark as clearly as by daylight, and
that he had such auctioneer-hammer strength of
knuckle that with one fillip of his fingers he
could knock down a page and break his head
into the bargain; which only proves what an
admirable modern critic his imperial majesty
would have made, being such an adept in the
summary demolition of pages. And though very
recondite and ingenious, the world has not derived any great benefit, or even an additional idea,
from Hippocrates' account of the Macrocephali,
or race of people with long heads—a race which
indeed is still extant on the other side of the
Tweed.

That "*rien n'est beau que le vrai*" is the *truest*
truth that ever was uttered; and as light was
sublimely said by Plato to be the " shadow of
God," so is SIMPLICITY, the shadow or evidence
of TRUTH, and the real test of greatness of
mind. About the sham and the assumed there
is always a glitter, a *faux brillant*, an *effort*, in
fact, *de se faire valoir*, to *appear*, where to *be* is
impossible. Monarchs wear diamonds, gold, and
ermine, but the tinsel, cut glass, cotton velvet,

and cat-skins of their mimic reprefentatives on the ftage, are of neceffity lit up and fet off with all forts of falfe lights to dazzle the vulgar, and to *feem* like the reality for which they would fain pafs. All this is the difference that ever has and ever will exift, between gilding and gold; but had there been no gold there would be no gilding, and this, like all other fhadows,

> " Proves the fubftance true."

The ambition to *attain* and to *appear*—that is, the angling for the opinions of men, with the femblance, or at leaft with the infinitefimal fragments, of virtues and eftimable qualities, where, with half the fame trouble we might in reality poffefs and practife them, is the infallible fign of an empiric, whether in an emperor, an author, a private individual, or a pfeudo-philofopher. Now this ftraining after appearances and wifhing to *feem* great, was efpecially the cafe with that " meaneft of mankind" (and his brilliantly lacquered and gilded intellect) my Lord Verulam. As Tacitus fays of Vefpafian, he was *omnium quæ diceret aut ageret arte quadam oftentator;* that is, he had a certain art of fetting off all he faid or did, with a fort of oftentation; or like Corbulo, whom the fame honeft hiftorian reprefents as *fuper experientiam fapientiamque etiam fpecie inanium validas*, namely, that befides his wisdom and experience, he made every trifling appearance become prevalent. Now, setting aside one's knowledge of the utter hollowness and corruption of Lord Bacon's character, but on the contrary, giving him the benefit of supposing that he fully acted up to the straight geometrical line of worldly probity and prudence that he inculcated in his writings, still it *is* but *worldly* straightforwardness and prudence, derived from the very narrowest, shallowest, and most mundane source; and you may read him forever by his own bright and perfectly well-trimmed patent lamp, and never feel the slightest love for or going out towards the man; your head unequivocally agrees with him, but your heart never communes with him for the best of all possible reasons—that he *has* no heart to commune with. Even the very fire he takes from the altar, in *his* hands is but a pale borrowed taper; for his religion (?) such as it was, was but an adoption of the last, and best, discovered lubricative for the STATE MACHINE—the decent and expedient covering for a cold heart and an attenuated soul. Incapable of love, he was equally impervious to friendship,[1] but the *theory* of the thing is of

---

[1] Such men as Lord Bacon have tools, flatterers, and what he himself would have called "followers;" but how could he (surcharged as he was with his own egotistical worldliness), possibly have felt friendship? For truly says Montaigne,

course to be reduced to proper worldly maxims, emanating from, revolving round, and reverting exclusively to SELF. And so he writes a tame, bald Essay "ON FOLLOWERS AND FRIENDS," and sets out with the following highly-prudential axioms:—

"Costly followers are not to be liked, lest, while a man maketh his train longer he maketh his wings shorter. I reckon to be costly, not them alone which charge the purse, but which are wearisome and importune in sutes [suits]; for ordinary followers ought to challenge no higher condition than countenance, recommendation, and protection from wrongs;"—with a great deal more of such well-weighed, purely selfish, and one-sided considerations, all of which might be summed up into the following apothegm:—

WITH REGARD TO THE WANTS, SORROWS, HOPES, FEARS, WRONGS, RIGHTS, FEELINGS, AFFECTIONS, OR WELFARE OF YOUR FELLOW CREATURES, INVARIABLY MAKE YOUR OWN IN-TERESTS THE FILTERING MACHINE.

How different is all this self-worship and self-

"Friendship is a sacred thing, which can only arise between good men;—exists only by mutual esteem; supports itself, not so much by services on either part, as by goodness of life. That which makes one friend certain of another, is the knowledge that he has integrity; the sureties which he has for him are his good disposition, fidelity, and steadfastness."

patenting from dear old self-forgetting and self-abnegating Michel de Montaigne!¹ With a mind as immeasurably beyond Lord Bacon's, as the Andes or Mount Olympus are above Primrose Hill. It never enters into his wise, simple, honest head to be proud or vainglorious of the stupendous capacity God has given him; for inasmuch as it *was* the gift of Omnipotence it appears to him as much a matter of course as his eyes, ears, hands, feet, or any other of the compound parts that make up the man called Michel Montaigne. The mind, the wondrous mind, he merely keeps well tended and cleared, as *the* light the same beneficent Creator has given him to guide him on his apointed way, and keep him in the right path. In his every act, in his

---

¹ Montaigne has been falsely called an egotist, because he had so much sincerity and so little vanity, as without reserve to show the shreds and cross-grains of his mental hangings, as the obliging Gobeliners do of their tapestry to inquisitive visitors, after they have been charmed and instructed by the rich colouring and graphic epics produced by these curious ulterior workings. But egotism, properly so called, belongs to the odious moral, or rather grossly immoral, attribute of selfishness. Of this most Stygian and polluting of all vices, the kind-hearted old Gascon gentleman's ever prompt and primary consideration for others, whether his friends, his equals, his inferiors, or his superiors, proved that he had not a particle. And as for the mere constant repetition of the pronoun "I," that is unavoidable in essay-writing, which is a sort of physiographic autobiography.

every thought, without any flourish of trumpets in the way of professions or fine sentiments, you *feel* that he *knows* that the MORAL, and not the INTELLECTUAL, is the lever of life—a lever whose fulcrum is in ETERNITY! His religion is neither a form, a sect, nor even a creed, so much as a deep, pure, subtile essence, a sort of angel leaven, which, while it causes his nature to rise above the earthly dross with which the best of human things are kneaded, at the same time curbs all his higher attributes into the most profound abnegation, the most unquestioning and child-like submission, to the Giver of those attributes; and even if he cannot suppress a smile at some of the nominal miracles of mediæval Italy, how quiet, how tolerant is that smile! for he knows that all such are but garbled legends of God's great concrete miracle of creation!

Never had a man, and still more a genius, so little of the *ego* in him. Whether he is giving a *festa di balla* and silk aprons and gauze head-dresses to the peasant girls at Della Villa (the baths of Lucca), taking a hint how cheaply he may improve his beds at Montaigne and those of the poor on his estate, or regretting he did not bring a cook with him that he might have picked up the knack of some of the quince soups and other nondescript *plats* he mentions,— all his wishes and actions have a spontaneous reference to the well-being or pleasure of others, and are jotted down in the same simple, truthful, unostentatious way, with no fictitious motives assigned to them, and no finishing touches of either style or sentiment, so that they may appear to the more advantage in the Great Exhibition of publication. Then he honestly owns the badness of the Italian, in which his diary is written, for he has not the least wish or intention to impose the fiction on the public that he can write Italian as fluently and correctly as he does Latin or French, but only wrote in Italian, as he says, to exercise himself in that language, honestly regretting that during his tour he had associated too much with his own countrymen to make·all the progress in the *lingua toscana* that he wished. My Lord Bacon would have either re-written it in Latin or choice Elizabethan English, put the bad Italian into the fire, or else have had it remodelled by some Roman *savant*, and so duly quartered with his own acquirements,—learning a cross, pretense, *fitchée*, humbug. I have always had a theory, and Montaigne confirms it, that the greatest minds are constructed upon the same principle as an elephant's trunk ; that is, that while endowed with the strength and necessary power to raise and master the greatest things, they are at the same time gifted with a delicacy and minuteness of perception, for observing and picking up the fmalleft. And fo we find Montaigne, on his journey through Germany, Switzerland, and Italy, quietly locking up the great laboratory of his mind, putting the key in his pocket, and with all the accuracy of the moft perfect, thrifty, and notable houfewife, obferving and retaining the flighteft novelty and improvement in domeftic economy, were it only in the mode of airing linen, drefling a trout, or placing a faltcellar on a table ; for he knew too much, not to know that it is of *little* things that that wondrous arcana that we call " life" is compofed. There would be no globes if there were no globules. The analytic chemift is by far the fubtleft. The moft fcientific workmen are employed for the minuteft portions of watches and all other machinery. The fineft lace, with its endlefs mob of bobbins and maze of almoft invifible threads, is wrought by folitary women underground, left the air fhould fnap the threads (which are themfelves like woven air, fo impalpable,) and thus mar the defign which is fo beautiful, and though fo complex, in its details, fo fimple in its effect, as a completed whole. Why then cannot the delicate threads attached to the clumfy and more oftenfible bobbins of this great (and to our ignorant and uninitiated eyes) complicated lace pillow of creation remain in their places, and truft to the guidance of the fkilful hand that knows how beft to move them? Why all this bother about "woman's million?" Woman's million, like woman's sphere, is EVERYWHERE, though she has but ONE ORBIT, and that is, her HOME. True, she may, by the injustice or brutality of man, be shot from out that orbit, in its most stringent and conventional sense, and often have we cause to regret in the present day,

> —— " that women, whose price is so far above rubies,
> Should fall to the lot of such brutes and such boobies;"

but what then? A true woman, like a bee, can find and hive sweets, and make a home anywhere, whether in a garden or in a desert. " Woman's million," like man's million, is *to do her duty in that state of life into which it has pleased God to call her.* They may not, indeed, in many instances have any witnesses to their fulfilment of this glorious million, or, as the case may be, martyrdom, besides that God who has appointed it; they may not even have the homœopathic *douceur*, the small Victoria medal, a biographer, to chronicle either their million or their martyrdom; for more Doctor Johnsons than are known, have lived and died, without a faithful Bozzy to make a double-entry of all the good things they said and the better things they did; and whole circulating libraries of Miss Brontës have been relieved from life's hard tread-

mill, without benefit of a Mrs. Gafkell to perpetuate the manner in which they pealed potatoes
and the meritorious manner in which they did
not "eat mutton cold," but converted it into a
hafh for dinner. But neverthelefs, all and each
of thefe very important little things, which make
up their great account, *have* been duly entered,
depend upon it, in the imperifhable Doomfday
Book above. Now don't let any woman who
does me the honour of reading thefe pages fuppofe for one moment that I am preaching up
the limited liability houfehold drudge fyftem for
women. God forbid! In a general way, it is
their ignorance that is their infirmity; the more
they know (mind, I don't fay that they *pretend*
to know, *or wifh to be thought to know*), yes, the
more they know, the more they'll *do* and the
better they'll be. Some women, if in a garret, a
cellar, or more horrible than either, the cabin
of a fhip! contrive to fill it with a happy and
HOME atmofphere, which is a fort of Claude glafs,
that beautifies the worft profpects into a pleafing
view. I knew an Englifh lady once, who, after
all her life being ufed to every luxury, was con-
demned to three fmall rooms in a continental
hotel. She was not exactly popular among her
compatriots. Who is poor in purfe, and not
equally poor in fpirit? Infolence, with money,
is independence; but independence of character

without money is pride. Moreover, the miſſes
called her a "blue," becauſe ſhe was guilty of
knowing a little more than they did; the men,
becauſe ſhe was not a flirt nor a worſhipper of
their hereditary ſuperiority, proſcribed her as "a
ſtrong-minded woman," and

"Calomniez, calomniez!—il en reſte toujours quelquechoſe,"

as Scribe ſays; ſo I confeſs I was attacked with
the epidemic prejudice againſt her; for I do not
like blues, bores, or *ſo called* ſtrong-minded
women, any more than I like arſenic, ſtrychnine
or oxalic acid; only I have lived long enough to
know, that in this great drug mart, the world,
poiſons are often by miſtake labelled Simples, and
vice verſâ ; but for one perſon who inveſtigates
the matter for himſelf, ten are poiſoned by
nominally innocent preparations, and twenty
avoid innocuous panaceas from their ſuppoſed
deleterious qualities, owing to the undeſerved
bad name beſtowed upon them. But ſo it has
been ever ſince the world's dentition. Our eyes,
which ſeldom deceive us, are rarely if ever con-
ſulted; while our ears, which have been filled
with falſehoods ever ſince his Satanic majeſty
was co-reſpondent in Paradiſe, are generally im-
plicitly believed. Once, and once only, did I
hear anything like enthuſiaſtic praiſe beſtowed
upon this lady, and that was by a Frenchman,

who, upon hearing her duly diffected by a countrywoman of her own, fired up and faid—

"Non, non! elle eft charmante; à côté de l'efprit elle n'eft pas anglaife, et .puis, c'eft la meilleure pâte de femme que la terre aît porté; elle fait du bien à tout le monde, d'autant plus, qu'elle *fait comment le faire.*"

And then, twirling his mouftache and turning to me, who fat next to him, he faid—

"Tenez, madame; je vous dirais deux mots charmants d'elle."

He then told me that one night, at Madame Récamier's, Châteaubriand had knocked down with his elbow a little Sèvre cup belonging to a *déjeuner*. He was in defpair at his awkwardnefs, but Madame Récamier made light of it, and faid it was of no confequence; whereupon Mrs. Greville, the Englifh lady in queftion, faid, turning to Châteaubriand—

"Ah, monfieur! on voit bien, que madame n'eft pas *Atala*, car elle ne met pas fon bonheur en chaque taffe! (*Chactas.*)"

"C'eft tres-joli, n'eft ce pas?" faid the Frenchman; to which I fully affented.

He then told me the other, which was, that he met Mrs. Greville at dinner one day at the Princefs L——'s. On going into dinner the fandal of her fhoe broke, and the Ruffian Prince,

G——, who was taking her in, seized it, and putting it into his waistcoat pocket, said—

" Ce petit brin de ruban sera le roman de ma vie ! "

The hostess, hearing the word " roman," turned round and asked—

" De quel roman parlez vous, Prince? "

To which Mrs. Greville laughingly replied—

" Du dernier roman de Soulié, madame."

This was quite enough, and as the only thing I resolutely avoid is a fool, be it male or female, I resolved that I would call upon Mrs. Greville the next day. I did so, and after ascending the usual number of dirty stairs and encountering the *obligato* mosaic of atrocious odours indigenous to continental hotels,— of which that greatest of all abominations, stale tobacco smoke, is the *alpha* and *omega*—once within her rooms, the atmosphere was that of Arabia Felix ; there was a delicate tepid perfume, floating, as it were, on the current of thorough fresh air that circulated freely through them. The first thing that struck you on entering was the appearance of intense and habitual comfort and the brilliant cleanliness. All the knickknackery was in such perfect order—the buhl blotting-books and desks polished as mirrors, the flowers so exquisitely arranged, the books looking what books ought to be—friends

and companions, and not merely stuck up, doing
company for the sake of their gorgeous bindings;
so that every English person that came in exclaimed, " Oh ! what deliciously cosy, comfortable
rooms !" and every foreigner, " *Ah ! comme c'est
soignee ! comme tout cela a l'air grande dame !*"
And yet poor Mrs. Greville had not even "a
maid of her own !" and on that account, though
so essentially and pre-eminently social, was obliged
to relinquish going into society. But all this
bien-être and elegant *entourage* were the daily
work of her own hands. If you dined with her,
though she never gave you but two things, they
were perfect of their kind ; and there was no
continental tagrag and deficits in the arrangements of the table—the glass, plate, and linen
all having the same brilliant luxury of cleanliness ;
for she had broken in one particular waiter and
chambermaid to her ways. So true is it that
some persons have the happy art, not only of
seeming but of *being* more generous with sixpence
than others can be with a hundred pounds ; because generosity consists in the feeling and the
manner with which a thing is bestowed, and
therefore is it, that the *obolus* of a really liberal
nature, will always *win* more good will than a
miser's thousands can *purchase*. When I knew
Mrs. Greville more, I found out that I could
have backed her against all the nurses of Scutari

in a fick room, and that in the confeétion of a
fhirt or a *falmi* fhe would have eclipfed the beft
chef and fempftrefs extant ; and although, added
to all this, the woman *was* guilty of being able
to argue with you from Ariftotle or expound to
you from Epiétetus, "pedantry" remained in her
diétionary and was to be nowhere to be found in
her ; for I never knew a more thorough and *femi-
ninely* feminine W oman in her habits and *ways,*and
the depth and delicacy of her feelings; fo much fo,
that no one would have ever fufpeéted that fhe was

> " learned, fave in gracious houfehold ways.
> Not perfect, nay, but full of tender wants;
> No angel ; but a dearer being, all dipt
> In angel inftinéts : breathing Paradife,
> Interpreter between the gods and men."

Withal generous and felf-facrificing, as *only*
women *can* be, and what, had fhe been a
man, would have been called "*the* beft fellow in
the world !" But the alchemy of comfort in
which fhe was fo pre-eminently fkilled, and which
is one of the effential parts of " woman's miffion,"
arofe from her fcientific knowledge of and artiftic attention to detail, or *fmall things*—which
are the *primum mobili* of all great ones. Ar-
chimedes moved the greateft weights by the fimple
contrivance of three or four ordinary pieces of
timber joined together, but the fecret confifted
in the *order* and the art of their combination.

The greatest events in life, for good or evil,
whether for nations or individuals, if traced to
their source, will be generally found to have
arisen from the *smallest*, and therefore apparently
the most insignificant, causes. And truly says
Cicero, in his fifth Philippic, *Quis nesciat mini-
mis fieri momentis maximas temporis inclinationes?*
namely, Who does not know that the greatest
variations of time proceed from the minutest
moments? Women, however, like Mrs. Greville, who *quietly* do their duty in that state of
life into which it has pleased God to call them,
ay, and do it even to the inanimate things about
them, neglecting nothing, must resign themselves to living un*pronée* and dying unchronicled.

Que voulez vous? The greatest heroes are
often born with a *valet de chambre* appended to
them, and the greatest bores with a Bozzy. But
courage, true-hearted women! Remember, that
when Bethulia was to be delivered from the army
of Holofernes, God did not employ mighty and
steel-clad warriors, but He "*broke down their
statelinefs by the hands of a woman.*" What has
been, may be again.

But to return to Montaigne. The greatest
charm of the man to me is, his *reality*. He writes,
not to gain a reputation, nor even to assume
the superiority of teaching his fellow-men, but
because the deep well-spring of thought is *there*,

and muft gufh out ; and *that*, confidering the
perilous and bigoted times in which he wrote,
with a pure, undefiled, and fearlefs honefty, is
beyond all praife. And this genuinenefs and
guilelefs fimplicity pervaded his whole character.
For in his journal, when he fpeaks of the ova-
tions he received in his travels, it is always with
a little innocent fort of humble vanity, as if he
thought it *fo* good and kind of the people ; and
never dreamt of arrogating any compliment as a
juft debt to his own merits; fo that one can
almoft fancy one fees the reflection of his half
pleafurable half modeft blufh on the paper
when he adds, " But no doubt it is their cuftom
to offer thefe courtefies to all ftrangers of a ·cer-
tain rank." Of the immeafurable fuperiority in
calibre, depth, breadth, and originality of Montaigne's mind over Lord Bacon's there can be no
doubt; and as far as mere learning goes, which is
not intellect, but merely the food of intellect, there
is a greater and deeper fource of it in *one* of
Montaigne's effays, to fay nothing of the pith
and marrow of *true* wifdom, than in all Lord
Bacon ever wrote. Like the golden thigh of
Pythagoras, mentioned by Diogenes Laertius,
but which Plutarch tells us in his life of Numa
was a mere charlatanic ftratagem of the philofopher's [!] to convey to his admirers and the
vulgar, (who conftitute the ballaft of all artificial

celebrity,) an impression of his divinity, so my Lord Bacon, if duly weighed in the scales of impartiality, will be found to have given us more golden thigh than golden rules.

To gauge the minds of the two men, it is only necessary to recall Lord Bacon's Capel-Court-Minories maxims,—how to avoid risking our own welfare, interest, or comfort in any way for our friends, and how always to make use of them without giving them any chance of returning the compliment (*here*, at all events, the great man, the peripatetic of the golden thigh, *practised* what he preached!)—you have only, I say, to recall these crooked, hard, worldly maxims, and compare them with Montaigne's friendship for and devotion to, the memory of Monsieur de la Boëtie. There is nothing on record more true, more perfect, or more beautiful, than the former, or more tender, touching, and constant, than the latter. The truly great are those, not whose writings make us wiser in the world's shallow lore, but those whose lives make us better. Great, then, is the debt that the world owes to thee, oh! MICHEL DE MONTAIGNE! for after a life spent in life's best humanities and kindliest links, who ever left a lovelier example, not so much of the ruling passion as of the ruling virtue "strong in death" as thou didst? For we are told that shortly before his death, his tongue becoming paralyzed, he could not speak; so writing down to have all his servants called in, he got out of bed, put on his dressing-gown, and when they were assembled *gave* them each with his own dying hands, the legacies he had left them, fearing that when he was dead, they might be put to inconvenience, trouble, or expense to obtain them. Ten minutes after he had conferred this, his last, act of considerate kindness upon them, he expired.

Verily this was better, nobler, greater, than the vain-glorious, arrogant, and therefore somewhat ludicrous pomposity of a man's bequeathing his own fame to the world, and after a time, to his country; for it was leaving his whole nature — that inalienable personal estate — to ETERNITY, and APPOINTING OMNIPOTENCE AND THE RECORDING ANGEL AS HIS EXECUTORS! The fruit and foliage are the visible, and sought-after portions of a tree, but its and their vitality is in the roots; and the *morale* is the root of humanity. It is for this reason that the merely intellectual, however transcendent, is but an air-plant, that has no radical source of duration. Thus the world outgrows its Mirabeaus, Bolingbrokes, Humes, Gibbons, and Voltaires, which are but so much head-gear, the fashion of which changeth and passeth away; but the world, or rather human nature, never outgrows its Shakespeares, Senecas, and Montaignes; because such minds are the pulses and arteries of its great universal heart. Goethe, if we take the mere measure of his brain, was of larger calibre than Schiller; but the moral organization of the MAN, being cold, shallow, and defective, dies with his body, and finds no embalming process in the hearts of his fellow-men, as Schiller did, when once his light had gone out. For posterity is just; and it is always THE WHOLE MAN, and not the mere brain, that it dissects. Therefore, all honour to *thee*, now and evermore, wise, good, subtle yet simple, profound, clear-minded, nice-conscienced, broad-hearted, MICHEL DE MON-TAIGNE!

AN OLD MAN'S SAYING.

I HAD once a grandfather; indeed I believe the thing is *not* uncommon, though it is the fashion to say that some persons never had one. Be that as it may, I'm sure no one ever had such a dear old lovable grandfather as mine was. I'm not going to sentimentalize over him. Heaven forbid that I should so mock the manes of the noblest nature and truest heart that ever issued from the Maker's mint, and which, when called in, returned to it, with the Sovereign's likeness and superscription in no way defaced or corroded by their long currency among men. No, I'm not going to sentimentalize over him, for *he* was no sentimentalist,—fortunately for himself, and more fortunately still, for those belonging to him. For your professed sentimentalist is generally a finished scoundrel, or at best a frothy theorist, totally devoid of affections and principles.

Besides, about sentimentalists as about all other charlatans and pretenders, there is generally a spice of pomposity, and my grandfather had not an atom of that Bœotian buckram about him. His manners (the most finished of the old school, which *had much* artistic finish about it,) were far too bland, easy, polished, and high bred, to have the slightest taint of the *parvenu* rigidity of pomposity in them. It was not on account of his being the hero of a hundred fights, his having conducted several embassies and missions to a successful issue, or the broad ribbon of the Bath that glowed across his ample chest, the stars of half the European orders that formed a galaxy on his breast, the freedoms of cities in their gold boxes, the sable pelisses and the diamond snuff-boxes he possessed in sufficient number to have put away each of his own virtues separately in, nor even his brilliant and truly classical wit, that lightened in his eyes before it flashed from his lips, which stamped him so unmistakably for what he was—A THOROUGH GENTLEMAN, but the genuine, genial, and practical Christianity of his whole life, that made him the idol of those two justly judging extremes—YOUTH and AGE.

Many men have not only a fine outline but an amiable quality of character; but they lack the minute Flemish painting of detail, the womanly anticipatory kindness of *little* things, the gentle glidings of true unfelfifh goodnefs, which is feen and *felt*, but is too noifelefs to be ever *heard*. And thefe my grandfather had, more even than any *woman* I have ever known. He did not hang up his cremona behind the door at home, like many other celebrated performers in the *rôle* of *beaux efprits* in fociety, but with an inexhauft- ible fund of anecdote, chiefly gleaned from his own ftirring and eventful life, had always the *mot pour rire;* he was juft as racy, brilliant, and agreeable *en petit comité*, with us children on a fummer lawn, or by a winter firefide, as he would have been among all the magnates of the land. For he was at once a realization and an incarna- tion of Bifhop Hall's axiom, that "Love and action do necessarily evince each other. True love cannot lurk long unexpreffed: it will be looking out at the eyes, creeping out of the mouth, breaking out at the finger's ends, in fome actions of dearnefs; efpecially thofe wherein there is pain and difficulty to the agent, profit or pleafure to the affected. O Lord, in vain fhall we profefs to love Thee if we do nothing for Thee! Since our goodnefs cannot reach up unto Thee, who art our glorious head, O let us beftow on Thy feet (Thy poor members here below,) our tears, our hands, our ointment, and whatever other gifts or endeavours may teftify our thankfulnefs and love to Thee in them."

With the moſt joyous and genial nature, that diffuſed itſelf like ſunſhine over all around him, yet, in the great fellowſhip of human ſorrow and human ſuffering, was he ever foremoſt. His firſt *thought* was always how he could either ſerve, ſave, or give pleaſure; and, as in fire-arms, the report follows the flaſh, ſo in his moral arſenal the deed ever followed quick upon the thought. Truly his whole life was a redemptive conflict to a glorious and eternal victory! For ſhall not thoſe who ſuffer for, and with their fellow pilgrims, and thus ſerve their God as He has ordained here, reign with Him hereafter? Yea, verily, as ſurely as yon golden ſun that ſets to-day ſhall riſe again in glory to-morrow!

Dear old man! not only is thy ſhadow leſs on this bleak cold earth now, but few other ſubſtances are there, worthy to replace even that beneficent ſhadow which never *darkened* any threſhold; but with a holier and more tempered light, ſuch as an angel's wing might do, laden with glad tidings.

But heaven knows beſt; let none diſpute it. My grandfather lived and died juſt as, and when he ought. He could never have got on in the preſent day at all. The ticket-of-leave ſyſtem of politics alone, would have driven him mad; for he had ſpoken in Parliament when oratory was the *thing*, not the *word;* and patriotiſm was deemed a *fine quâ non* for its foundation; and when *his* voice woke the senate, he had had Europe for an echo, and Edmund Burke for an auditor and a panegyrift. Neither am I at all fure that the literature, or rather the *literati,* of the prefent day would have fuited him; for, as he was fully capable of appreciating the improvement in the *former,* and the degeneration in the latter, he would have been continually deploring, that where fuch an immenfe floating capital of undeniable talent of a very high order exifts, the owners of it had not the fame advantage as that attributed to Terence by an old writer, who, in fpeaking of the graphic and vividly life-like delineations of character and the unctuous humour of his comedies, thinks that his chief merit was owing to his having had the good fortune to have Scipio and Lælius to give his *dramatis perfonæ* " the true turn of gentlemen."

But above all, this prefent time would not have fuited my grandfather, nay, it would have been pofitively antipathetic and antagoniftic, to him, from its being a utilitarian age, that generally walks, no matter how dirty the ways, moftly in highlows, and *always* with its breeches pockets clofely buttoned. It never *fays* either a foolifh or a rude thing, but it alfo never *does* a kind or a civil one. It goes about giving lectures to the great unwafhed, for it is an old and a true faying, that words coft nothing ; whereas the fmalleft modicum of foap (with the exception of foft-foap), would neceffitate at leaft fome trifling globule of pecuniary outlay. It takes up ftarving wretches for prefuming to beg, but it never begs any meafure to prevent them ftarving. It builds, Bibles, miffions, magnifies, preaches, and *profeffes* Chriftianity ; in fhort, does everything but *practife* it. Our philanthropy, which, like our preferves, *ufed* to be confected at home, is now all done abroad, in joint-ftock, companies, limited (and *very* limited too), *via* ragged fchools, penitentiaries, fhoeblack brigades, anything and everything that can enable us to buy our benevolence in the cheapeft market, and blazon it in the deareft. But to hope for one *individual* touch of fympathy, or even common humanity, from thefe wholefale charity-mongers, would indeed be like the futile tafk of attempting to extract funbeams from cucumbers, as a fingle ftiver from thefe profeffional Samaritans' [?] *own* coffers is never forthcoming. On *principle*, they never do anything of the kind ; for this is a commercial country, where *intereft* and principal are very properly infeparable ; and unknown, anonymous individual fympathy (that had not been organized into a committee, or incorporated in a fat commiffionerfhip), would be *interfering in private affairs ;* and beftowing a fixpence that did not flow from the tributary ſtreams of public contribution, would be encouraging idleneſs and vagabondiſm, and is ſhocking, immoral, and not to be thought of—and ſo it never *is* thought of.

Alas for my poor primitive, unphiloſophical, and monetarily immoral grandfather! though he did ſubſcribe largely, to all the hoſpitals and public charities, yet there were, as there ſtill are and ever will be, ſo many ſharp, keen, yet ſhamefaced neceſſities, that never come within the pale of public munificence, ſuch myriads whoſe rags have been *once* fine linen, who cannot dig, and who to beg are aſhamed, that ſomehow or another my grandfather's hand was never out of his own pocket; but what it took from thence, ſo far as its owner was concerned, always remained a myſtery between himſelf and the God in whoſe ſervice he beſtowed it, and although

"Open as day to melting charity,"

that ſaid right hand of his, was the only cloſe ſecretive thing about him; for I verily believe its ſiſter hand quitted *this* world, in total ignorance of the ſplendid collection of light hearts and bright faces, it had ſo laviſhly bought; till their final account was audited in the next. But the gifts of that hand (and a beautiful one it was, by-the-by, as if to bleſs and to give were

all it had been created for, and that, confequently, it had done naught elfe), unftrained as
thefe gifts were, they were but the fpray and
fprinklings, from that inexhauftible fountain, his
pure, deep, illimitable heart. When I look back
upon the quiet beauty of that old man's life, I
envy him not fo much even for all the good he
did, as for the *way* in which he did it, he fo
thoroughly underftood the art; but then, to be
fure, it was his whole ftudy. If it were only to
buy a toy for a child, or a trinket for a young
girl, he always took the pains to fift out the
identical toy or trinket that was moft wifhed
for; and any affair he undertook for others,
however intricate, tedious, or even hopelefs,
he was not fatisfied to wait till fome tangible
bufinefs point had been achieved, to communicate
with thofe for whom he had undertaken it; for,
as he himfelf was wont to fay, all bufinefs is
flow, but fufpenfe is feverifh and wayward; and
moreover, to thofe who fuffer and hope, and
ftill more, to thofe who fuffer and fear; minutes
feem hours, hours days, days weeks, weeks
months, and months years; and fo he filled up
the great defolate fpace between expectation and
fruition, with kind words of fympathy and hope.
This would have been *real* goodnefs, even had
he been an idle man, with a large furplus of
golden leifure to fpend as he pleafed; but he

was not, for, although an habitually and conſti-
tutionally early riſer, every minute of his twelve
hours had its appointed work ; and though I
have often heard him complain of not having
had time to anſwer the letters of very great per-
ſonages as immediately as his nice punctilio of
good breeding deemed right, yet I never knew
him not to *make* time, to anſwer, or to take the
initiative in writing to, thoſe who were in any
way diſtreſſed " in mind, body, or eſtate ;" ſo that
it was a high compliment (and we felt it and
meant it as ſuch) when my couſins and ſiſters
and myſelf ſaid his dear, honeſt, noble, handſome
old head reminded us of Nep's. Nep, or Nep-
tune, was a big Newfoundland dog, at once our
idol and our victim, and the " guide, companion,
friend," of the whole family. Only Nep's handſome head was black, with merely a white mark
up his forehead, that we uſed to call a ſalt-ſpoon ;
and my grandfather, continuing the faſhion of
his day, wore powder ; but it was the ſweeteſt of
all violet powder, with a ſubſtratum of peculiarly
fragrant jeſſamine pomatum, which Pendrel, his
old valet, who had been with him in all his
campaigns, would have thought ſacrilege to have
got anywhere but where he had got it for forty
years,—at Smith's, in Bond Street. Never to this
day does a ſoft breath of violets and jeſſamine
ſigh through the air, without bringing the tears

to my eyes, and all my youth back to me, with
its long funny viftas, and that dear old grandfather, and Nep, my mother, coufins, fifters,
all! peopling them as vividly as of old. Such
magical and myftical "open fefames" of memory's moft fecret cells, are the "linkèd fweetnefs"
of both mufic and perfumes!

But tufh! there is no ufe in my going back
all this way to meet thofe who never can return
to meet me here. Would that I could hope to
be worthy of meeting them hereafter! And yet,
were juftice alone to gauge God's goodnefs, dare
the beft amongft us hope? But between the
twin feraphs—Mercy and Faith—the worft need
not defpair.

When I began this paper I merely intended
to have recorded one faying of my grandfather's,
but truly, "Out of the fullnefs of the heart the
mouth fpeaketh." So now let me make up for
loft time, by recording that golden faying, or,
I fhould rather fay, rule, of his,—which I have
never forgotten; and may all who read it here
never do fo either!—which is one of the beft
wifhes I can offer them.

It was on a gufty evening in September, we
were at Richmond, in one of thofe pleafant
houfes clofe to the Park. There were no railways in thofe days, but admirable pofting (worth
them all, except for fpeed), and long ftages and

short stages, and mail coaches, and pack-horses, and canal-boats, *et voilà tout*, and no penny postage, so the twopenny post was thought a great deal of, and considered one of the greatest boons and improvements of modern times. It was, as I before said, a gusty evening in September, and we children, with the dessert (for there were no *diners à la russe* in those days), had just made our appearance. Now, if my grandfather *had* a fault, it was that he was a bit of a coddle; but no; it was not a fault, it was an aversion, that he shared in common with all old people, to draughts, night air, and moving immediately after dinner. Just before dinner, he had despatched cousin Robert, Meg, and me, in preference to a servant, with a note to a poor gentleman of the name of Trevor, a half-pay captain, who, with a wife and four children, was lodging over a bookseller's shop in the town. I suspect the note contained a somewhat more flimsy inclosure, for my grandfather always wrote upon very thick-ribbed wove paper, and used envelopes, which at that time nobody else did, except, perhaps, old Lord Hertford, the Prince Regent, and the persons immediately about him. Not that for a moment I mean to class these with nobodies,— their physical greatness alone, and the immensity of evil they did in their generation (which we in ours are now paying for), would preclude my doing fo. And fo, from the thicknefs of the paper, I could not be fure about the inclofure, for Robert had orders to fend it up by the fervant and wait in the fhop for the anfwer, that he might not in any way intrude on the Trevors. But from the tears that were in the poor gentleman's eyes when he himfelf brought us down the anfwer, I long after fufpected that there was an inclofure,—for at the time, child-like, I thought nothing about it. Juft as we returned with the captain's miffive the letters *viâ* the evening's poft were brought in, and amongft them was a long official document, "O.H.M.S.," with a large War Office feal on it. My grandfather, who was in the act of raifing a glafs of wine to his lips, put it down, and haftily broke the feal of the long blue parallelogram.

"Come! that's capital!" he exclaimed. "Bring me my hat, great coat, and gloves," faid he to the butler, from whom he had juft taken the letters, as the latter was about to leave the room.

"Surely, my dear father," faid my mother, "you are not going out! more efpecially on foot?"

"Tut, tut! that am I," rejoined my grand-father, rifing as he fpoke.

"I can tell you it's blowing what you call great guns, fir," put in Robert, longing to begin upon the walnuts without incurring the delay of any exodus.

" Why, my dear child," faid my grandfather, addrefling my mother, " I muft go, to give poor Trevor the good news before it cools and he fees it firft in the *Gazette* to-morrow. Fancy! the poor fellow has got his majority, and the appointment at Corfu alfo; fo now he 'll do!"

" I 'm very glad of it; but furely a fervant can go? or Robert will go again," remonftrated my mother.

" No, no; I would not mifs the fellow's face when he hears of it," faid my grandfather, " for a Field-marfhal's baton! For *I* never held out any hopes to him, and *he* was *quite fure he* never fhould get either his promotion or the appointment."

And this was faid with a long face, a fhake of the head, and a deep figh, in ludicrous imitation of poor Captain Trevor, which fet all of us children laughing.

" Well, but grandpapa," faid I, " you can go and tell him to-morrow morning."

" Child!" he cried, turning fharply round, and laying his hand with fome force on my fhoulder, fo as to imprefs his words, as it were, " you are a good girl enough, in your way, and though not likely ever to injure your health by too clofely poring over your books," (I was then twelve), " yet, I fuppofe you know what the copybook fays, that ' PROCRASTINATION IS THE

THIEF OF TIME?' Well, *I* tell you that it's *worſe*, for it is often the MURDERER both of opportunity and of thoſe whoſe hopes and lives hang upon very ſlender threads. So remember, my child, if you wiſh to be all *en régle*, and have your paſſport properly *viſé* for your final journey, for which none of us know how ſoon the *route* may come—

"NEVER PUT OFF TILL TO-MORROW THE MAKING A SAD HEART GLAD, IF IT CAN BE DONE TO-NIGHT."

SERVANTS.

CICERO relates that the ugliest and most stupid slaves in Rome came from England. Moreover, he urges his friend Atticus *not* to bring slaves from Britain, on account of their stupidity, and their inaptitude to learn music and other accomplishments. Cæsar also describes the Britons as a nation of very barbarous manners. In another place he remarks, "In their domestic and social habits the Britons are regarded as the most savage of all nations."

> " But, pray, young England, don't your sires despise,
> For just *such*, *you* seem, to many modern eyes."

And so, my young friends, you are likely to appear in the eyes of Europe, till each individual Briton can resolutely resolve to shuffle off his national arrogance and self-sufficiency, and strenuously apply himself to *individual reform;* for believe me, manners, next to morals, are the moſt important ingredient in the great ſocial *olla podrida*, and like hard eggs in a *mayonnaiſe*, unleſs they be blandly blent with the other nominally more important items, but mar them all by *their* ſingle failure. And general rules and wholeſale ſyſtems never will achieve this equal and moſt deſirable amalgamation, for each ſepa-rate adjunct requires a ſpecial and individual caſe. You want morally, what Herodotus tells us the Egyptians had phyſically: "Each phy-ſician," he ſays, "applies himſelf to ONE diſeaſe only, and no more. But all places abound in phyſicians; ſome are for the eyes, others for the head, others for the teeth, others for internal diſorders." And it is impoſſible to mix with any grade of Engliſh ſociety, without feeling how much, how very much, the MANNERS DOCTOR is needed for the community at large; for every one, with the few and rare exceptions that prove the rule, ſprouts his or her own thiſtle, and alas! *Non inultus premor.*

And this being the only thing *piquante* about the ſaid ſociety, unfortunately does not render it the more agreeable. And moſt decidedly, no claſs requires the MANNERS, and above all, the MORALS DOCTOR, ſo much as the ſervants—or rather, the no-ſervants of the preſent day—who poſſeſs in a pre-eminent degree all the diſqualifi-

cations attributed by Cicero to their anceftors;
the flavery only entirely left out, as they are
much more nearly related to a certain Cuffy upon
an American planter's eftate, previous to the
abolition of the infernal inftitution of flavery
(that is, of chartered flavery, for *un*chartered
flavery, it is to be feared, will, like "the poor,"
never ceafe from the earth). Well, Mr.
Cuffy, that typical "nigger," upon being remonftrated with by his owner, calling him "A lazy
rafcal, who was afraid of work," replied with
equal truth and fimplicity, "Me not afraid of
work, maffa; me lie down and go to fleep
befide him." But thefe modern Englifh femi-
detached Cuffies, the prefent race of fervants, do
more than this, for they have a noble contempt
for work, and neglect it altogether; always, like
the Levite in the parable, "paffing by, on the
other fide." There can be no doubt that the
power of disfiguring paper with ink, and, as if
ftung into revenge by all the "fpelling bees,"
making a raid upon orthography, fupplemented
by the power of reading all their mafters' and
miftreffes' letters, and enabling "Lizer" to incite
"Sarer Jane," *via* the penny poft, to additional
malpractices and infubordination, mifnomered
"education," which has been beftowed upon
it, has a great deal to anfwer for, "a *little*
learning" being proverbially a dangerous thing,

whether derived from the *Pierian* or the parish
spring. But the chief "origin of evil," so far
as the female class of domestic servants is concerned, is the want of those admirable vanity
safety-valves, sumptuary laws, which would provide and enforce a neat, decent, and becoming
costume for them, and prevent their exaggerating
what is already a hybrid between a nightmare
and a caricature, *i.e.* each succeeding hideous
fashion, the present most unbecoming and in-
decent *sortir du bain* style of dresses having
caused even a new Shakespearean reading, which
says:—

> " There is a tide in the affairs of men,
> And a *tied back* in the affairs of women !"

For dress, however ugly, trumpery, and disfiguring, is always *costly* to every class, according to
its means, or *want of means*, for indulging in it.
And the high priest which enables the " servant
gal" class to sacrifice to this Moloch is, Dis-
honesty ; for there are a hundred ways of being
dishonest, without resorting to the straightfor-
ward and perilous one of putting hands into
other persons' pockets, or abstracting bank notes
from their desks or *escritoires ;* such, for instance,
as making their employers pay toll upon everything that comes into their houses; purchasing,
both in food and all other articles, the cheapest

refufe, and charging the higheft price afked for the beft things ; in fhort, ftrictly carrying out the late Sir Robert Peel's commercial axiom, a very fupererogatory one, fo far as England is concerned, of "always buying in the cheapeft and felling in the deareft market." But the very worft, and to their employers moft ruinous, to their mafters and miftreffes, or rather as things now are, to their flaves and dependents, is, their want of knowing *how* to do the commoneft things, either in the fhape of houfehold or needle work, in the firft place, and their idlenefs in the next, as they live on and for excitement alone, *via* conftant "outing" and excurfion trains. Their worft and moft ruinous difhonefty, I maintain, arifes from their total neglect ; which caufes everything entrufted to them, whether plate, glafs, china, linen, books, or furniture, to go to deftruction. But all this, fills their exchequer for the three or four months they condefcend to ftay in a place, and *via* the faid trumpery drefs and the eternal excurfions, to provide their *one* aim in life, a "young man," whom they literally "pick up" and marry, without a farthing in their pockets or the moft latent power of earning one in their head, or hands, or habits, fo as to make anything like a *home* for themfelves or the "young man." And hence all the horrible and fummary wifemurders, from drink and defperation, caufed by

dirt, diforder, and domeftic difcomfort. Formerly, no one would think of taking a fervant
who had lived *only* fix months in a place; now,
that is thought a long term; and as to a character from their laft place, they are quite inde-
pendent of *that*, either by falfe ones, or through
thofe focial pefts, called "fervants' regiftry
offices," whofe fole *raifon d'être* is to fleece both
the hirer and the hired, and who know nor care
nothing for either. Formerly, fervants had at
leaft, good, honeft, induftrious mothers, who
before their daughters ever attempted to go to
fervice, taught them their place, if they could
not teach them their bufinefs; and above
all, took care to inculcate the golden rule of
"fubmitting to thofe in authority over them,"
and alfo habits of thrift, with fufficient induftrial
knowledge to enable them to make and mend,
their own clothes. Now, thanks to fewing
machines, and other royal roads to idlenefs, they
do not know how to thread a needle, much lefs
how to ufe one; and afk the rector or curate
of any parifh, and he will tell you the fame
ftory; with variations, it may be, but the motive
is invariably the fame, *i.e.*, that if he give to
the mother of an almoft ftarving family half-a-
crown of a Saturday evening, it is *not* food it
will be transformed into, but fome coarfe imitation of a flower, or a rat's-tail of a feather for

the eldeſt girl's hat, to enable her to look additionally vulgar and diſreputable on the following day at church. Naturally, *je prêche pour ma paroiſſe;* for having for thirty years had the good old thorough-bred, well trained, efficient, truſtworthy, devoted ſervants, overflowing with gratitude for what was *leſs* than their due, and who lived with me till they died, the preſent extreme of incapacity, vulgar inſubordination, and black ingratitude, was really too great a ſhock to ſoul, nerves, and body. Formerly, when I eulogized, as in common juſtice I never was tired of doing, the good qualities and devotion of my ſervants, I was met with, "Oh, no wonder you have good, truſtworthy, and devoted ſervants; ſee how kind and how liberal you are to them." Now, when I complain of their incapacity, inſubordination, and the not being able to humaniſe, much leſs to buy them at any price, the anſwer is, "No wonder; you ſpoil, and are too generous and too indulgent to them, and the common Engliſh nature never underſtands that ſort of thing, more eſpecially as they don't meet with it elſewhere, and ſo they only take advantage of you in every way they can, thinking it is folly, and not kindneſs, which makes you act in ſo exceptional a manner."

This *is* verifying Prior's lines with a vengeance!—

"Gently touch and smooth a nettle,
It will fting you for your pains ;
Ufe it rough, as man of mettle,
And it folt as filk remains.
'Tis the fame with vulgar natures—
Treat them kindly, they rebel ;
Ufe them rough as nutmeg-graters,
Then the rogues will treat you well."

But, confidering that fo many of the *foi-difant*
ladies (?) of " the period " have adopted the language of fervants and all the verbal kitchen ex-
otics, it is not much to be wondered at that the
tone of their minds fhould, as a natural fequence,
fink to the fame calibre ; for when one hears
what, according to their focial pofition, fhould
be gentlewomen, fay to a fervant, " Tell *Cook* I
fhall dine at feven," or, " Tell *Coachman* I want
the carriage at two ;" or when they ring the bell,
fay, " Coals, *pleafe*," or " Tea, *pleafe*," and call
going in a carriage or cab " *riding*," or call needle-
work by the generic term of "fewing," or perfume by the intenfely vulgar and peculiarly
fervant's-hall name of " fcent," it is not, verily,
much to be wondered at, that, in hiring a fervant
for a friend, by way of courting popularity with
the very low upftarts who now call themfelves
fervants, inftead of impreffing their duties upon
the nominal fervant, they fhould lower their *foi-
difant* friend in every poffible way, by faying,
" This lady is very fidgetty,"—the kitchen term

for any miſtreſs who exacts order and obedience in her houſe,—" But *you* muſt *put up* with that, and I'm ſure you'll find it a good place upon the whole." One of theſe " ladies" with the minds of laundreſſes, having got a cook for a friend, which cook turned out a confirmed drunkard and thief—which was no poſſible fault of the lady who hired her, but only her misfortune, juſt as, if ſhe had turned out perfection, it could have been no merit of this lady's, but merely a fortunate coincidence—yet, when another friend tried her hand, and got for her friend another cook, who turned out a worſe thief and drunkard than the former one, inſtead of expreſſing any ſympathy or commiſeration to her friend for her continued trouble and diſappointment, the high-minded and amiable view the firſt lady took of her friend's uncomfortable poſition was to rub her hands and ſay, " Ah ! I'm glad others cannot ſucceed any better than I did !" Verily " Lizer " or " Sarer Jane " could not have ſaid more !—though even *they* might have ſaid leſs.

Next comes the exceeding ſtuckupativeneſs[1] of theſe ſtarving waifs and ſtrays from cellars, gar-

---

[1] A lady, a few evenings ago, ſpeaking upon this peculiar phaſe of the " ſervant gal " craze upon " the genteel," in which they even ſurpaſs Mr. Towle, told an amuſing anecdote of the letter-bag being opened one day at breakfaſt, and, among the other contents, was a letter on pink paper, directed " To Miſs

rets, and back lanes. They are too fine to carry a parcel, were it only the fize of a penny roll, and did the fate of an empire depend upon having it immediately, and no matter how great the lofs to their employers. Of courfe it was not *their* fault; for they are all popes as to infallibility, and kings that can do no wrong. They ordered it, and the tradefpeople promifed to fend it directly; fo what more could *they*, the fervants, do?

This reminds me of two ftories. One a friend of mine told me whofe grandfather was Bifhop of ———. She faid, going through the hall one day, he heard a tremendous fquabbling, and very loud excited voices in the lower regions; and upon inquiring the caufe of the butler, who had juft announced that the carriage was at the door, he was told that fomething was wrong with the oven; and the cook having ordered Bridget the kitchen-maid to take a certain venifon pafty, that could not be baked at home, to the baker's, that young lady had flatly refufed to walk through the ftreets fo encumbered. Whereupon, the bifhop ordered both the delinquent and the pafty, to come to him. Then, telling the carriage to wait till his return, he marched the blufhing Bridget in Indian

---

Jemima Jenkins, Efqr." (!) This turned out to be for the kitchen-maid; feeing her mafter's letters fo directed, no doubt fhe had informed her correfpondent that this was the "*genteel thing to do,*" and exacted this tribute to her focial ftatus.

file before him, took the pafty himfelf, and carried it in great ftate to the baker's, as if he had been walking at a coronation, with the crown on a velvet cufhion. The legend further tells, that Bridget never again refufed to carry pafties or anything elfe to the baker's, and even carried *her-felf* in a much more becoming manner ever after.

The other ftory is better known, being of Rowland Hill, who told his coachman to go every morning to a farmhoufe, at about a mile's dif-tance, for the milk and cream for breakfaft. Whereupon that functionary refufed, with much offended dignity, faying that that was not *his* bufinefs to do. "Oh, I beg your pardon," faid Rowland Hill; "then may I afk, what you do ftrictly confider your bufinefs?"

"Why, to drive the carriage, fir."

"Oh, very well! Then have it at the door every morning at half-paft fix punctually; and drive Mary the houfemaid to —— farm for the cream."

Formerly no girl thought of going to fervice until fhe had learnt at leaft the rudiments of houfe-hold work from her mother, which even the pooreft mother, in thofe days, was capable of teaching. Now, they iffue ready dreffed out, from their cellars, garrets, or back lanes, knowing *literally* nothing, and quite determined they won't be taught any thing, and think it "very *ard* they are told fo often the fame thing;" but it never

enters their heads to think it at all hard for their
miftrefs to have to tell them the fame thing fo
often. When I firft married, it was one of my
ways of trying to ferve my fellow creatures, to
take girls out of the village when in the country,
and have them thoroughly well trained under the
houfekeeper in all the ufages of houfehold work,
and what is equally effential, taught the quiet,
refpectful manners of a fervant; and *then*, but
not till then, they fought a place, afking but little
wages at their firft fituation, and gradually afking
more as they improved in capability and deferved
more. Now, every dreffed-out flattern, who has
never lived in fervice before, and is confequently
obliged to own that fhe knows nothing of houfehold work, but modeftly adds fhe has no doubt
fhe can do it all if fhe tries, begins by afking, or
rather demanding, £20 a year;[1] which *ufed* to
be the wages one gave one's own maid, fkilled
in drefs-making, hair-dreffing, and all the other
duties belonging to her department. The pre-

---

[1] Now though it is unfortunately quite true that houfe
rent, taxes, and every fpecies of food, groceries excepted, are
three times as dear as they were twenty, and twice as dear as
they were ten years ago, yet the only two things upon which
maid-fervants fpend their money, namely, trumpery drefs, and
excurfion trains, on the other hand, are twice as cheap as they
were at either of the above-named periods; fo that there is
no valid reafon, or even plaufible pretext, why their wages
fhould have increafed fo prepofteroufly.

sent housemaidenly *débutantes* also lose no time in
stating most stringently and specifically, *their* requirements as to hours of rising, going to bed,
and their Sundays out ; with other holidays, and
being allowed to see their friends, which of course
means their " young man." Being, thank heaven,
once more in smooth waters, with excellent servants, which I am happy to find still *can* be had,
clean, competent, obedient, trustworthy, and
attached, I can laugh, though not without a re-
trospective shudder, at the bitter trials I have had
in this way. One gigantic drum-major in petti-
coats that I had, was of such a diabolical temper,
with such a vulgar Billingsgate way of showing it,
that she frightened not only me but the whole house,
and did not even know how to sweep a carpet
properly ; and as I had for many years a first-rate
housemaid, who was in fact a perfect furniture
doctor, and had secrets for keeping oil-paintings,
carvings, bronzes, mirrors, and all sorts of *bric-à-
brac* in perfection, I told the drum-major all these,
and insisted upon having all my things kept up as
they had always been; at first she resisted, doing
so in the most insolent manner; at last, when she
found how my ways of doing things simplified
her work, and abridged the time it took, she con-
descended to say one day, " Yes," or as she pronounced it, " *Yaas*, I don't say but what your way
is the best, for I see it is now." "That," said I,

"is not the point; beſt or worſt, I chooſe to have things done in my own way in my own houſe." Added to her inſolence, ſhe was very ungrateful and equally diſhoneſt, and ſo offenſively rude to every one, that I threatened to report her conduct to the lady who had recommended her to me as a treaſure of honeſty, and good temper!

" *She* did not care for Mrs. ——, nor for me, nor for any one; and *ſhe* was not going down upon her knees to people with that cringing civility that the other ſervants did!"

" Ah," ſaid I, "you had better kneel to God, and pray to Him to change your heart and temper."

" God's nothing to me!" was her horrible anſwer.

" I fear not," I replied.

While another *lady* of the ſame genus, upon my daring to tell her that ſhe ſhould not have let one of the bed-room fires go out, clenched her fiſt and ſtamped her foot as ſhe vociferated, " Ah! the gentry will ſoon get no ſervants at all, and be obliged to do their own work,—that's what we are trying for!"

" We have to do our own work now," ſaid I, "and to pay ſervants very dearly at the ſame time for not doing it; but don't you think, for your *own* ſakes, ſo long as you condeſcend to take our money and eat our bread, it would be better, and more to your own advantage, if you conducted yourfelves a little more confcientioufly? I am not for one moment faying that you are not quite as good, or even a great deal better, than we are; but *that* has nothing to do with it. Suppofe the pofitions were reverfed, and I was obliged to become your fervant to-morrow; there would be no earthly ufe in thinking what I was born to, or what I had been accuftomed to; you would then be my miftrefs; and though all my ways would be very different from yours, it would not only be my duty but my intereft, in return for the food and wages you gave me, to endeavour to pleafe and conform to your requirements in every way that I could, inftead of raifing a ftandard of rebellion at every order you gave me."

Well, this amiable democrat ended by going upon the ftreets, and the drum-major got a place with a falfe character, which at all events muft have been better than her real one.

Another young lady—alfo, of the genus houfemaid—living in a clergyman's family, having let her mafter out, was about to refaften the hall door, when his little boy, who was in the hall, faid, " You need not do that, Jane, for your mafter will be back directly."

" Who do you mean by *my mafter?*" cried the Amazon, turning fiercely round and glaring at the child.

" Why, papa, to be fure."

" He 's not *my* mafter, he 's my employer ! "

While a young lady at a National fchool in the country, who was wafting her time over a little bit of ufelefs crochet, which fhe had converted into a fort of cotton blackamoor, which never could be fcrubbed white, while her ftockings were well ventilated with large holes ; upon my faying to her—

" Now Mary, inftead of wafting your time upon that perfectly ufelefs crochet, don't you think it would be better if you mended your ftockings ? "

" Pleafe um, mother don't like me to mend ftockings ; fhe fays as it ain't *gen*-teel."

All this infubordination and ftuckupativenefs combined it is, which is the moral dry-rot that is fapping the foundations of fociety. What all England requires to be taught, the higher quite as much as the lower orders, is, that Work is about the moft ennobling thing in the world ; and as *every* fort of work *muft* and ought to be done,—there is in reality no fuch thing as "menial work"—that bogean myth, which middle-clafs vulgarity fo dreads. The only really menial, and therefore degrading things, are, idlenefs, ufelefsnefs, dependence, fhams, fubfitutes, brag-gadocia, and worldlinefs ; which latter, is the nucleus of all vulgarity—Vulgarmindedness.

HAPPY JACK.

THERE can be no doubt that the flat-
nefs, ftalenefs, unprofitablenefs, and
inanity of Englifh life arife from its
block machinery fort of uniformity,
and total want of individuality in thought, action,
or character; its echo and follow-my-leader fort
of conventionality, which caufes anything like
originality or independence of opinion or action,
in the rafh perpetrator of either, to pafs for
mad or bad; and be tabooed accordingly. Unlefs
indeed the faid individual happens to be exceptionally rich, as every thing is "*for the million*" now-a-days, whether financially or focially
fpeaking, or elfe placed on the pinnacle of
the world's flippery high places; *then* indeed,
eccentricities, however outrageous, or vices,
however flagrant and notorious, not only pafs
unchallenged, but are cited with laudation, as
proofs of genius and fuperiority, and ferve to

form additional hecatombs of truth and juſtice to the foul national fetiſh, PUBLIC LIFE! which, ſo far as politicians go, might be deſcribed in the identical words of the keeper of a menagerie, who addreſſed a ſchool of young gentlemen as follows:—

"This ere hanimal, my little dears, is a leopard. His complexion is yaller, and agreeably diwerſi-fied with black ſpots. It vos a wulgar herror of the hancients, that the critter vos hincapable of changin his ſpots; vich vos diſproved in modern times, by obſerwin that he wery fre-quently ſlept in one ſpot, and next night changed to another, cordin as it ſuited him beſt."

And there is ſomething ſo exceptionally petri-fying in the whole arcana of political life, that the American epitaph upon the miſer who died of ſoftening of the brain, would do admirably for that of moſt "diſtinguiſhed members of the legiſlature," viz.:—

"His head gave way, but his hand never did. His brain ſoftened, but his heart never could." But leaving all this block machinery, let us go into the highways and byways, and ſee if we cannot pick up ſomething like character, freſh-neſs, and originality, among the weeds and wild flowers, that are hedged within their little ſpheres by the roadſide. It ſo happened, that in walking the other day to Foreſt-hill I was caught in one

of thofe drenching fhowers, that have been fo
prevalent during this fevere fummer of 1876.
But fortunately there came rattling by, a return cab, which I ftopped, and got in. The
man drove me to my deftination, at Foreft-hill,
where I remained about half-an-hour, the cabman having, to my great fatisfaction, driven his
horfe and himfelf, under the fhelter of a hofpitable
archway. On my return, long before I reached
my own gate, the fky became blue and cloudlefs,
and

> " No fun upon an Eafter day
> Is half fo fine a fight "

as that fun was, playing bopeep with the haw-
thorns and acacias and among the white horfe-
cheftnuts and the glorious rich red Spanifh cheft-
nut bloffoms. So that, being particularly ftruck
by the gloffy coat, and, for a hack, the unufually
fat fleek fides of the bright bay, full-fized, high-
ftepping cab-horfe, I ftopped to pat him and give
him fome green boughs, as he was trying to
gather a falad for himfelf; then, turning to the
cabman, I complimented him upon the high condition of his horfe, which, as I told him, was
much to his credit, as it fhowed what good care
he took of him.

" Ay; care in courfe I takes on him," faid he,
twirling a ftraw in his mouth. " But care be
blowed! It ain't *that* as does it; it's his mind."

Thinking a horse "with a mind" ought to have a name, I asked, "What do you call him? what is his name?"

"Well, his *crissen* name is Jack, but I calls him 'Happy Jack,' for 'tis his mind as does it; for he's *that* contented and happy in his mind, that if he war fed upon tenpenny nails and pack-thread, he'd be in better condition than any ofs in England. Yer see he don't never let nothink put him out, don't Jack; he just takes the world as it goes."

"As most cab-horses do," I put in.

"Ay, but that don't pervent Jack having pinions of his own; but he keeps 'em to his self, and takes the world as it goes."

"In short, he don't, let his *pinions* fly away with him?"

"That's about it. Jack knows what's what, but when he comes in *contac* with them as knows nothing, he never interferes with their little stock in trade."

"Truly a wise horse, a most wise horse; and like all wise heads, he has a silent tongue in his."

"Then yer see, 'tain't only his mind, but he can eat hany think "——

"That he has a mind to?" I put in.

"No, hany think; gloves, boots, horange peel, money—hany think "—spreading the two florin pieces I had just given him on the palm of his hand, and offering them to the omnivorous Jack of the great mind, and corresponding appetite.

"Ah," faid I, "nothing eafier than to eat money; but, poor fellow, let him eat his, in oats, and don't make him fwallow thofe."

"Why not? I allus tells him as he's the beft right to the money, as he arns it; but carrots is *his* turtle and wenfon, only there ain't none worth eating now but French ones, and they's dear."

"Well, tell me where Jack's ftable is, and I'll fend him a hamper of French carrots."

"Ho! will yer though? well, I'm uncommon obleeged to yer! That's fuft rate!"

"I will indeed, for I think very well of you, for being fo fond of your horfe."

"Fond on him! I fhould think fo. The parfon fays it's wicked, when I fays my miffus and the kids is all very well in their places, but that place is not afore Jack; for in pint of clevernefs they are not fit to hold a pail of water to him. Then yer fee, this is the way on it: I fticks up all the more and thinks a deal the more on him, hon account of hall the lies, hill natur, and defamation he's fubjec to hon account of my mates being henvious of him and me; they never have a good word to fay of either on us; they tells my fares that I fhall upfet the cab, that Jack's a roarer, and that he jibs!"

" Well, they fibs," faid I.

" And no miſtake! Did yer ever fee water through a folar *mikerſcope*, marm?—with all them devils let loofe, a devouring, a running down, and a tearing on heach other to pieces? Vell, *that's* the world to a hair; fo no wonder fo many poor critters wiſhes, and takes theirſelves out of it."

In my own mind, I fo perfectly endorfed the truth of the cabman's ſimile, that I thought it better to end this philofophical *ſéance* with a Burleighan nod of the head to him, and another pat of the fat fides of that " paragon of animals," Jack. But there was fuch quinteſſential truth, in what this poor man had faid of his compeers' ufage of his excellent and therefore much calum- niated equine friend, that it fet me thinking that the world's opinion of moſt perfons, is as various as that of hiſtorians and biographers, on that of Edward Lord Clarendon, who was alternately deified and defamed for party purpofes. Southey declares him to have been the wifeſt and moſt upright of ſtatefmen, while Brodie does not heſi- tate to reprefent him as a miferable fycophant and canting hypocrite; and Hume, on the other hand, embalms him with the greateſt refpect and admiration. Hallam is cautious and timid in his praife,—that worſt, becaufe leaſt honeſt, fpecies of condemnation. Agar Ellis unheſitatingly pro- nounces him an unprincipled man of talent. The

old ſtory of the chameleon, might greatly aid a
correct ſolution of theſe divers contradictory
opinions, both as regards public and private
characters; and thus award to each ſeparate and
oppoſing verdict its quota of truth. But in the
midſt of much that is dubious in all ſuch matters,
one thing at leaſt is certain, and that is, that none
of theſe judgments individually, no, nor taken all
collectively, can ever hit upon the true inter-
dependencies and ſequences of events, at all accurately; any more than they can upon their origin.
And how ſhould they? Since the *real* motives
of our actions are for the moſt part ſo ſubtile
and concrete, as to become, even to ourſelves, a
"great firſt cauſe, leaſt underſtood." But all
theſe are only pſychological experiments *in cor-
pore vili*, alias human nature; ſo, to return to the
nobler, becauſe the more innocent animal, the
poor cab-horſe,—the next morning, his devoted
ſlave, alias his maſter, came for his hamper of
carrots. "Happy Jack" indeed! to whom happineſs was ſo eaſy! Unlike the world's little great
men, to whom hampers of kingdoms, make happineſs impoſſible.

MACAULAY.

I WISH I had the honour of knowing Mr. Trevelyan perfonally, that I might have the pleafure of thanking him *vivâ voce* for the immenfe boon he has beftowed upon *me individually*, irrefpective of my being one of the atoms that make up the world at large, by his publication of "The Life and Letters" of his exceptionally gifted and diftinguifhed kinfman, the really great Thomas Babington Macaulay. It is given to fo few of us here below, to complete the cycle of our thought, and ftill lefs, to realize that of our *ideal*, that what greater boon can one human being beftow upon another, than the proofs that one at leaft of his or her golden idols had *not* feet of clay, and that, though albeit of coloffal dimenfions, the ore was pure and unalloyed from fummit to bafe? And this is precifely the incalculable fervice which

Mr. Trevelyan[1] has juſt rendered me. I never was, even in my "ſalad days," much addiɛted to hero-worſhip; I believe thoſe who live much among what are called "celebrities" ſeldom are, they being too nearly in the ſame category as ſupers and ſcene-ſhifters in a theatre, who ſee too much of the ugly machinery, paint, and tinſel, to be capable of winding themſelves up to admiration point at the fineſt and moſt glittering transformation ſcene ever produced; however marvellous the effeɛt may be upon thoſe outſiders, called "the public," who know or ſee nothing of the *modus operandi*; but—

"In that ſoft amber light of long ago."

From the very firſt appearance of "Knight's Quarterly Magazine," wherein I made Macaulay's acquaintance—alas! only in print—the cultus I then and there offered up at the altar of his genius, has gone on ſteadily increaſing in devotion, as in the courſe of time diſcrimination has been grafted upon enthuſiaſm. It was on "A Night in Ancient Rome," that I firſt meet him,—that gem *par excellence*, from the antique, ſo wondrouſly and clearly inciſed to the moſt delicately minute touches, ſo exquiſitely and highly poliſhed, not only externally but inter-

---

[1] M.P. for the Border Boroughs.

nally, that even he himſelf, though ever working
up to the ſame pinnacle, never ſurpaſſed it.
Poor Praed, too, ſo charming as far as he went,
the "Vivian Joyeuſe" of "Knight's Quarterly,"
confirmed me in my new creed, and told me I
did not and could not overrate Macaulay, and
promiſed that ſome day he would make him
known to me. Woe is me! that "ſome day," like
ſo many other "ſome days," never came. Had
he lived perhaps it might. Well! who knows,
but in the "good time coming," which never
comes on this ſide Styx, all our days may be
theſe happy long due "ſome days?" Of courſe
it did not need Mr. Trevelyan's upon the whole
very able life of his illuſtrious uncle, to additionally ſpread the fame of Macaulay's *genius*
from pole to pole, but it *did* need it to ſet the
ſeal of genuineneſs upon the MAN—the hall-mark
upon his virtues—which, though outlined very
plainly, even through the dazzling effulgence of
his great intellectual ſolar light, could not, of
courſe, be verified in detail. It was impoſſible
to read a ſentence Macaulay ever wrote or ſpoke,
even in that great arena of humbug, and ſham
Areopagus, St. Stephen's, without *feeling* that all
was what it profeſſed to be. Even his wondrous
and unapproachable ſtyle, was as natural and
ſpontaneous, as the ruſhing water-worlds of
Niagara, or the rich gorgeous fertility of tropical

vegetation. You *felt* by intuition that he did not, as it is called, " get up" the fubject ; but that it was all the infallible refult of the richnefs of the indigenous foil, evenly, carefully, and fcientifically handled and cultivated, then fown with endlefs variety of the choiceft and beft kinds of feed, which only required the genial auxiliaries of time, feafon, and atmofpheric influences, to produce their inevitably luxuriant crops; where it was fo manifeft that to the planting of Paul and the watering of Apollos, God had fo glorioufly and unlimitedly given the increafe.

Yes, in all he wrote, in all he faid, in all he did, you felt that the greatnefs, that is, the goodnefs, of the man was genuine; *he* could not *act* a part, becaufe the one, nature had intended him to create in the world's drama was too noble a one. Like all fingle-minded, broad, deep, natures, he had the courage of, not only his opinions, but of his likes or diflikes, in great things or fmall, with the ftream for, or againft it. This it was, which caufed him never to lofe an opportunity of denouncing and detecting, that arch-charlatan and vulgar-minded felf-feeker and felf-worfhipper, Henry, Lord Brougham; or of proclaiming amid any amount of fneers, ironical fmiles, and raifed eyebrows, his love and admiration of " Clariffa Harlowe." Of courfe it was only poor, patient, perfecuted Clariffa that he loved, and of courfe he had an equally ſtrong and laudable wiſh to have ſtrangled the whole of the Harlowe family, and have ſold Harlowe Place after, for a private madhouſe; and regretted that there was a chronological impoſſibility exiſting to prevent his having had the ſatisfaction of even ſo tardily having rid the world, of that typical fine gentleman, Mr. Lovelace. Nay, more, I have not the leaſt doubt that he not only would have endorſed but even had admired! deſpite the " Lays of Ancient Rome," that ſonnet " To the Author of Clariſſa," which appeared in the ſecond edition of Richardſon's beſt work:—

" To the Author of Clarissa.

" O maſter of the heart! whoſe magick ſkill
The cloſe receſſes of the ſoul can find;
Can rouſe, becalm, and terrify the mind,
Now melt with pity, now with anguiſh thrill.

Thy moral page, while virtuous precepts fill,
Warm from the heart, to mend the age deſigned,
Wit, ſtrength, truth, decency, are all combin'd,
To lead our youth to good and guard from ill.

O long enjoy what thou ſo well haſt won,—
The grateful tribute of each honeſt heart,
Sincere, nor hackney'd in the ways of men;
At each diſtreſsful ſtroke their true tears run,
And nature, unſophiſticate by art,
Owns and applauds the labours of thy pen."

But if Macaulay had never uttered or written a fyllable but the golden axioms contained in the following excerpt from Mr. Trevelyan's juft-publifhed " Life " of him, they alone, would have fufficed to immortalize him, as a practical out-come of his true and honeft nature, illuftrated by his own choice :—

" I often wonder what ftrange infatuation leads men who can do fomething better, to fquander their intellect, their health, their energy on fuch objects as thofe which moft ftatefmen are engaged in purfuing. . . . . That a man before whom the two paths, of literature and politics, lie open, and who might hope for eminence in either, fhould choofe politics and quit literature, feems to me madnefs. On the one fide is health, leifure, peace of mind, the fearch after truth, and all the enjoyments of friendfhip and converfation : on the other fide, is almoft certain ruin to the con-ftitution, conftant labour, conftant anxiety. Every friendfhip which a man may have, becomes pre-carious, as foon as he engages in politics. . . . . Who would compare the fame of Charles Townf-hend, to that of Hume ? that of Lord North to that of Gibbon ? that of Lord Chatham to that of Johnfon ?"

Yes; but the moft extraordinary infatuation of all is, that as the great ambition of this fort of men is *to live*, that is, to go down to pofterity,

they cannot comprehend that nothing *can* live
but what has life in it, and there is no vitality in
anything but the *real*, and alike for the moſt
exalted, as well as for the meaneſt intellect, their
daily and hourly chequered life, of hopes, fears,
duties, trials, ſtruggles, ſorrows, affections, diſ-
likes, temptations, the warring againſt them, or
ſuccumbing to them; in a word, each human
being's ſchool of ſelf-diſcipline is his *only real*
and immortal life, and not the adventitious external circumſtances by which he is ſurrounded,
whether they be the pomps and vanities or the
perils and pauperiſm of earth's lottery. But the
fact is, that worldlineſs is the moſt vulgar-minded
and vulgariſing, as it is nearly the moſt univerſal
of all vices; and like Death it enters everywhere,
for it is quite as often found on the higheſt rung
of the ladder, among thoſe born in the purple, as in
the ſuburban villa or behind a counter. A mind
like Macaulay's would naturally recoil from the
ſewers and ceſſpools of political life, but he was
only one of the few exceptions that prove the rule,
for there can be no doubt that PUBLIC LIFE is
the great *fetiſh* of England, and the wholeſale
ſacrifices made to it, and for it, are even more
unſpeakably and revoltingly hideous than thoſe of
its African prototypes. And what wonder? when
it is no matter how worthleſs, unprincipled, and
immoral a man's private or real life may be, *that,*

is completely ignored, and never for a moment
makes him ineligible for not only afpiring to but
obtaining the higheft pofitions in public life, which
only require a certain amount and verfatility of
brain power and unlimited moral elafticity.　For
half-a-dozen Macaulays in the world, who can
comprehend and feel that though, of courfe,
nepotifm and back-ftair influence can and do
beftow power and pofition, there are no fuch things
as real honours except thofe which have been
honourably earned or nobly won.　Yet I am fure
there is hardly a fecond, who would have had the
honeft fimplicity to have evinced his gladnefs as
he did, when his unfought peerage was offered
him.　Still, it was quite in keeping with the
whole tenour of his life, which was, to confer
benefits upon all who came within his reach ;
and verily, if any honour there were in this cafe,
it was moft unqueftionably all on the fide of the
peerage.

But public men, in their infatiable cravings for
what they imagine to be immortality [?] forget
what ironical jades the Fates are, and how TIME,
who ought to be old enough to refpect what fo
efpecially belongs to him, aids and abets them
in their iconoclaftic pranks.　The prefent and the
future have their intereft, at their refpective antipodes.　For inftance, if in thefe days of railways
and electric telegraphs, any one got a letter putting

him confidentially *au fait* of the projected "Royal
Titles Bill," five days, or even four-and-twenty
hours, before the newfpapers were on the fcent
of it, even if it did not afford any great delight,
or indignation, or intereft, to the recipient of the
letter, it would do fo as goffip capital for the
vifitors and neighbours of the favoured receiver
of the early intelligence. Yet juft put the dial
on two or three hundred years, and no one then
living will care one ftraw about the " Royal
Titles Bill," from the child that learns all about
it hiftorically as a tafk in the fchool-room, to the
child's parent, who liftens to it as a duty from
the child at fecond hand. But if, indeed, fome
private letters of this time fhould turn up, were
they only from Queen Victoria's real *femme de
chambre* (not miftrefs of the robes) to a fifter
Abigail in London, ftating that—

" Has her Majefty is to be made a Hemprefs,
which I don't confider no fuch great matter for a
Henglifh queen, taint as hif fhe was one of them
furreners, nor hif indeed as they was a going to
raife her falary with it, that would be a different
thing; but all I looks to his, that praps it will hadd
to *my* dooties confiderable, has of courfe the eads
will be wore higher than hever, and I not a
penny the better for it ; but hif there hain't that
'ere dreffing-room bell on the rampage again. I'll

write from Gummany next week. So no more at prefent, from

"Yours truly,
"DOROTHY DRESSER"

—this charming epiftle would excite more intereft and converfation from one end of the kingdom to the other, than the moft ftirring political events of the prefent day will in pofterity of three hundred years' growth. We enjoy, it is true, fo far as a laugh goes, that piece of ftale politics called "Queen Elizabeth's golden fpeech," *i.e.*, her laft to her Parliament, wherein fhe told them that all the glories and improvements during her reign, were due wholly and folely to her own wifdom and prefcience, but all the fhortcomings and mifcarriages "*were their culps;*" yet ftill *we* fhould now take much more intereft in hearing how many "Sirrahs" fhe beftowed upon her grooms for "*their culps,*" when fhe remounted her palfrey on her return to her palace, or how many "fwinging" boxes on the ear fhe beftowed upon her mifchievous maids of honour, when fhe difcovered that they had rouged the tip of her nofe inftead of her cheeks. And who, now-a-days, cares one jot for the political and public affairs in "The Pafton Letters"? One is glad, indeed, that Judge Yelverton's fpiteful pamphlet, trving to make out the Paftons were

villains, or *glebæ afcripti*, was eventually dif-
proved; and alfo, that though the Duke of
Northumberland did efcheat, or *tout bonnement*
cheat, poor John Pafton out of Caifter Caftle,
which bluff Sir John Faftolf had left him, it was
afterwards reftored to the family. But how
much more intereft does one take even in the
"worfted doublet which his wife Margaret
brought John Pafton from Worfted, when fhe
went to fee him in London;" and of which he
found the threads "almoft like filk." And moft
interefting are the parental outburfts of affection
in the fhape of "good thrafhings," regularly
twice a week, of Elizabeth Pafton, or the "head
broken in two or three places," from the fame
weekly allowance to her Aunt Margery. One
only regrets that there is not a graphic defcription of the *mife en fcène*, *i.e.*, the furniture and
dimenfions of the room in which this more than
monaftic difcipline took place; and likewife, as
they were fuch notable houfewives and "fkilful
leeches" in thofe days, that after their precious
balms had broken their children's heads, they do
not tell us what precious ointments they applied
to heal them. Their exact and refpective dreffes
and coifs, too, are great omiffions, as well as
the not clearly fpecifying with what implements
the caftigations were adminiftered,—birch, cane,
flipper, or cat? As for poor Margery Pafton,

"who fadly demeaned herfelf" by marrying
Richard Calle, a faithful dependent of the Paſ-
tons, and was turned out of the houfe for per-
fifting in her intention, by John the Second, who
faid that " Calle fhould never have his good
will to make his fifter fell candles and muftard
at Framlingham,"—I wifh I had been there to
have helped her in my little way, by giving an
order, not indeed that the gas fhould have been
cut off in the lower regions, feeing that in thofe
days they had none, but that nothing but tallow
fhould be burned in the Netherlands, that every
thing fhould be dreffed *à la tartare*, and that all
the maids (for of courfe the men would not
have fubmitted—they never do—to anything;
which proves their fuperiority,) well, yes, that
all the maids fhould have worn muftard plafters
en permanence, whether they had colds or not—
which, living in Norfolk, of courfe they would
have had, or ought to have had, all the year
round.

As for the abfence of all family affection
among us Englifh, that feemed to fo puzzle and
aftound all foreigners in thofe days, and caufed
the Venetian Ambaffador to doubt whether in
high or low life any Englifhman ever could have
been in love; I am fure we modern Englifh
have no changes or innovations in domefticities
to reproach ourfelves with.   Any little maudlin

family affection we may be encumbered with, there is always felf-intereft, like the Queen's Proctor in the Divorce Court, "intervening" to adjuft the balance; fo that

> "Love light as air, at fight of human ties,
> Plumes his light wings, and in a moment flies."

But, as we are alfo told that whatever abfence of affection there might be in the Englifh of the fourteenth, fifteenth, and fixteenth centuries, they were remarkable for their good breeding and extreme politenefs, this proves to us what a total lofs we *urfa majors* of the nineteenth century have fuftained. If there was any chance of infufing a little, even a few drops of this loft life-blood into them, one would almoft be tempted to recommend a courfe of educational vivifection, after the manner of the Paftonian weekly thrafh-ings and broken heads, for the rifing generation.

But as a more modern and illuftrious inftance of the vitality of reality reaching to immortality, in fact, the only well authenticated proof of the truth of the Darwinian theory of "the furvival of the fitteft," Macaulay's family muft, as a matter of courfe, be juftly proud of his genius and his fame, a pride that will defcend to his lateft pofterity; but for the immediate portion of it ftill living, I feel fure that, great and immortal as that genius and fame are, they are yet the two attributes

which, when recalling him, the family dwell on
leaſt. No, it is the kind, confiderate, ever ſym-
pathetic and affectionate friend, the large-hearted,
genial, many-ſided good man, who not only
thought of giving dinner parties to children in
his rooms at the Albany, for that would have
been nothing, but who invariably had the thought
and took the trouble of ſeeing that everything
was got that his little gueſts could poſſibly like.
Ah! great univerſal mother NATURE, there *you*,
as always, ſat enſhrined and paramount in the
heart, the deep, pure heart, of this great man,
though his intellect *was* brilliant-cut, and flaſhed
its myriad facets upon liſtening ſenates, and an
admiring world. No wonder, not that his family,
which was *his* nucleus, but that all who came
within the ſphere of his influence, loved him;
not, by all accounts, from any perſonal graces or
charm of manner, for it was ſaid that in appearance he was ungainly; no, it was the ſheer
triumph of mind, ay, and of ſoul, over matter;
crowned by that impalpable but ſubtle and
divine halo which goodneſs ſheds around all
who poſſeſs it.

I would have given more than I poſſeſs or am
ever likely to poſſeſs, to have been an inviſible
eye and ear witneſs to the ſcene of *his* "arreſt of
the five members"—I mean when the five irate
Quakers waited upon him at the Albany, to

expoftulate with him about the too life-like portrait he had limned of their idol William Penn.
" Its tone," as Mr. Trevelyan truly fays, "reminds
one of Johnfon," only from its conciliating effect
it muft have lacked the other leviathan's fledge-
hammerativenefs."

" I wrote," faid Macaulay, in reply to their
complaint, " the hiftory of four years, during
which he was expofed to great temptations;
during which he was the favourite of a bad king
and an active folicitor in a moft corrupt court.
His character was injured by the affociations.
Ten years before, or ten years later, he would
have made a much better figure. But was I to
begin my book ten years fooner or later for
William Penn's fake?"

" His vifitors," adds Mr. Trevelyan, " complimented him upon his courtefy and candour,
and parted from him on the beft of terms."

So I fhould fuppofe; but though Cæfar (Julius),
as Suetonius tells us, lacked the *vis comica*, and
therefore with all his greatnefs muft have been
but a dull fellow, Macaulay did not, fo it is *his*
face that I fhould fo much like to have feen,
after the departure of the five Quakers. If they
had only been " Friends in Council" and knew
how to keep their own, they might have known
before they came, that *their* Penn could have had
no poffible chance againft Macaulay's.

I am now glad that I did not fee his face, for it would have been that fupererogatory thing, an additional forrow, to be among thofe who

> "Ne'er can look upon that face again."

Truly,

> " His body is buried in peace,
> But his name liveth for evermore."

PROPOSED PLAN FOR A SUPPLE-MENTARY COLLEGE TO THE UNIVERSITIES,

FOR THE PURPOSE OF SAVING TIME AND TROUBLE WITH RESPECT TO UNDERGRADUATES LIKELY TO BE PLUCKED.

FOLLOWED BY TWO GHOST STORIES.

"THERE is a river," faith my friend Burton (not Burton-upon-Trent) "at the Swallow, that finketh into the earth and rifeth again two miles nearer Leatherhead. They do fay a goofe was put in, and came out again alive, though with the lofs of all its feathers."

This would appear to be a far fhorter and more fwimming mode of plucking than the ordinary procefs in ufe at the Univerfities, fo we ftrongly recommend that the propofed Supplementary Plucking College fhould be built at the *Swallow;* and the vicinity to Leatherhead is another congenial defideratum that would make the *pluckee* feel quite *en pays de connaiffance* at the little light dinner, given by Godfrey Nevil, brother to the great Earl of Warwick, in 1470, at his palace at York, to a few of his friends among the nobles, clergy, and gentry, wherein he fpent 300 quarters of wheat, 330 tuns of ale, 104 tuns of wine, one pipe of fpiced wine, 80 fat oxen, fix wild bulls[!], 1,004 fheep, 300 hogs, 3,000 calves, 3,000 geefe, 2,000 capons, 300 pigs, 100 peacocks, 200 cranes, 200 kids, 2,000 chickens, 4,000 pigeons, 4,000 rabbits, 240 bitterns, 4,000 ducks, 400 herons, 200 pheafants, 500 partridges, 4,000 woodcocks, 400 plovers, 100 curlews, 100 quails, 1,000 egrets, 200 rees, above 400 bucks, does, and roebucks, 1,056 hot venifon pafties, 4,000 cold venifon pafties, 1,000 difhes of jelly parted, 4,000 difhes of jelly plain, 4,000 cold porpoifes[!] and 400 tarts, 4,000 cold cuftards, 2,000 hot, 300 breams, 8 feales.

At this feaft the Earl of Warwick was fteward, the Earl of Bedford treafurer, the Lord Haftings comptroller, with many other noble officers. And there were 1,000 fervitors, 62 cooks, 515 fcullions, and innumerable turnfpit dogs. It is fad to add that in a few years after giving thefe agreeable little dinners (as will fometimes happen in more modern times), this poor gentleman fell into difficulties and died in great diftrefs, or as

the chronicle ſets forth, " The king ſeized on his
eſtate and ſent him priſoner into France, where he
was bound in chains[1] and died in great poverty.
Juſtice," concludes this Joſeph Hume of an
hiſtorian, "thus puniſhing his former prodigality."

But dear me! if we are to believe all, ay, or
even *half* we hear, the above little *ambigu* was
nothing to the way in which thoſe eccleſiaſtical
commons, the monks, ate, and thoſe *too well*
protected females, the nuns, drank.   Juſt liſten
to the requirements of a king's daughter and a
king's ſiſter in that way, according to Rymer.
As there was no *Times* newſpaper in thoſe days
with philanthropic advertiſers, anxious " to receive as inmates, Ladies [!], and Gentlemen of
intemperate habits," we muſt charitably hope
that in this inſtance it was not *in vino veritas*.

But here is the little item :

" In 1307," ſays Rymer, " Edward the Second
confirmed the grant his father, Edward the
Firſt, had made to his ſiſter, Mary, a Nun at
AMBROSEBURY, of 200*l. per annum*, 40 oak
trees for firing in her chamber,[2] and 20 *dolia*

---

[1] Like Lord Bateman, without, however, meeting with a
" Fair Sophia," which would not have been proper for an
archbiſhop, and altogether inconvenient in the event of his
being recalled from exile, as there were no coaches and three
in thoſe days to bring her back in, and the Church was his
legitimate bride.

[2] Surely it muſt have been too hot to hold her !

[or hogſheads] of wine, as long as ſhe continued in the Nunnery and lived in England.[1] And," adds the innocent Rymer, " the reader will not, I believe, be diſpleaſed to ſee the care that was taken in thoſe days for the *ſuſtentation* of the daughter and ſiſter of a king of England." Whereupon he gives the following ſtate paper : " The *King* to the *Sheriff* of *Wilts*, greeting.

" Foraſmuch as we are indebted to our deareſt ſiſter *Mary*, a *Nun of Ambroſebury*, in the ſumm of 12*l*. 7*s*. 3*d*. As well for hay, oats, litter, and ſhooing, as for her ſervants wages, whileſt ſhe tarried at *Windſor*, in the month of *December* laſt paſt, as alſo for her expenſes in travelling from *Windſor* to *Ambroſebury*, as in a Bill of our *Warderobe*, delivered by our ſiſter into our Chancery, appears more at large. We, willing to ſatisfy our ſiſter in the particular with all ſpeed we may, do hereby command you to pay to our ſaid ſiſter, or her lawful *Attorney*, the ſaid ſumme out of the iſſues of your Bailifry, without Delay ; and we in our accounts at your Exchequer ſhall make all due allowance for the ſame.

" *Witneſſe the King at* Windſor, Jan. the 1ſt, 1313.

           " By a *Bill of the* Warderobe."

---

[1] She muſt, in a meaſure, have infringed the contract by being often half-ſeas over.

But though I cannot, friend Reader, feaft you with a thoufand hecatombs like Godfrey Nevil, nor flufh you with twenty dolias of wine, like the royal Nun of Ambrofebury, yet I can, in order to "fpeed the parting gueft," act upon a fage axiom of another old chronicler, Ingulfus, who opined that " However dull a *Boke* might be at ye onfet, and even in ye maine parts thereofe ; it fhould not faile to have a *fpirate* in ye ende."

Therefore I fhall conclude with *two* fpirits, by giving you a brace of well authenticated ghoft ftories, as told to me fome years ago by the two ftill living actors in them, a lady and a gentleman, both of a certain age and pre-eminently *un*imaginative, or what is vulgarly called *not* given to romancing. One happened in broad daylight to an enthufiaftic difciple of Ifaac Walton, while angling the fultry fummer hours away. This I fhould have confidered unique, and therefore apocryphal, in the archives of ghoftology, except for the many ghofts who began to fee daylight about the reign of George I. according to Andrew Moreton, in that curious collection of fupernatural biographies of his, entitled " THE SECRETS OF THE INVISIBLE WORLD DISCLOSED, OR AN UNIVERSAL HISTORY OF APPA- RITIONS, SACRED AND PROFANE, UNDER ALL DE- NOMINATIONS, *whether* ANGELICAL, DIABOLICAL, OR HUMAN SOULS DEPARTED; with a great variety

of ſurpriſing and diverting examples never publiſhed before; alſo ſhowing how we may dif-
tinguiſh between the APPARITIONS OF GOOD AND
EVIL SPIRITS, and how we ought to behave to
them.

> "'SPIRITS, in whatſoever ſhape they chuſe,
> Dilated or condens'd, bright or obſcure,
> Can execute their airy purpoſes,
> And works of love or enmity fulfil.'—MILTON.

Sold by Thomas Worral, at Judge Coke's Head,
againſt St. Dunſtan's Church, Fleet Streeet.
MDCCXXXV."

The copper plates are not the leaſt curious
part of this book, next to the open and ſtraight-
forward proceedings of the apparitions; moſt of
which travel by fields, lanes, and gardens, knóck
at cedar-parlour windows at noon-day, are ſeen of
more than one perſon, and, moſt marvellous of
all, for the moſt part belong to *living* bodies,
who in order not to bear the brunt of their fantaſtic doings, go to great trouble and expenſe to
prove an *alibi* of ſeveral miles', and often ſeveral
hundreds of miles', diſtance, at the time their
ſpirits were ſo unwarrantably pawning their honour
and getting duplicates of their forms. But there
is not ONE in the Moreton collection, in my
opinion, half ſo wonderful as the two well authenticated, not to ſay "well-conditioned" apparitions, I ſhall now have the honour of preſenting
to you.

"There are more things in heaven and earth, Horatio,
Than are dreamt of in your philofophy."—HAMLET.

Place aux dames! even though we are going
fo much out of the world.   It is now fome five-
and-twenty years fince I became acquainted, in a
German town, with two fifters, of the clafs I de-
nominate "fenfible women," vulgarly called "old
maids."   They were not only fenfible, but, like
moft really fenfible people, extremely agreeable
and well-informed, the eldeft particularly fo, who
had for many years rubbed up againft Göthe
and Jean Paul, while fhe occupied a poft in the
little court of Weimar.   But if *fhe* had it in the
head her fifter carried off the palm in heart, for a
more thoroughly lovable, amiable, unfelfifh perfon
it would not be eafy to find ; but then, to be fure,
fhe had graduated in that moft humanizing and
mellowing of all fchools—affliction, and drawn
her fympathy for others, from the deep fource of
a great perfonal forrow ; not that there was any
furface fadnefs or even penfivenefs about her ;
on the contrary, her manner was *enjouée* and
prévenante, always ready to promote or join in
any of thofe thoufand little *jeux de fociété* which
pafs away an evening fo pleafantly, and which
French woman (for they were French, not
German,) fo pre-eminently poffefs the fecret of
making graceful as well as amufing.   Still, at

times, deſpite her cheerful manner, a deep ſhadow
would ſteal over her perfectly pale face, giving it
that intenſely deſolate and unearthly look which
a ſnow landſcape aſſumes when a gorgeous ſun
ſuddenly ſets, taking with it all the red and
golden roſes it had but the minute before been
ſtrewing on that wintry winding-ſheet. She always dreſſed in black, but merely rich black ſilk,
not mourning properly ſo called. Nevertheleſs,
ſhe had acquired the *ſobriquet* of "the widow,"
and the miſſes (for there *are* miſſes, even in
Germany, as well as ſentimental ſauſage-eating
Fräuleins), yea, verily, even the miſſes giggled
when they ſpoke of her as ſuch, and my curioſity
being piqued to know how ſhe had acquired this
honorary freedom of the conjugal ſtate, upon
inquiry I was told that thereby hung, not only a
romantic tale, but a ghoſt ſtory,—that Mademoiſelle Stéphanie de A—— had, fifteen years
previouſly to the time of which I am writing,
been engaged to be married to a M. Vander—
ſomething—a Dutchman. Everything was arranged, the day fixed, and they were to be
married in a month, when he was accidentally
drowned. To this part of the cataſtrophe it was
that the ghoſt ſtory was appended. Mademoiſelle
Stéphanie de A—— was in Hungary when ſhe
heard of the death of her *fiancé*, and for two
years after, on her return to ——, ſhe wore

deep widow's weeds, and hence her *ſobriquet* of
" *la veuve.*"

One Chriſtmas Eve that I was to paſs at the
De A——'s I found Mélanie, the eldeſt of the
two ſiſters, alone, arranging the Chriſtmas tree.
As ſoon as the ſervant who had been helping her
to decorate it had aſked her when he ſhould
light up the little tapers about it, and had with-
drawn, after extolling her taſte, ſhe and I went
into the other drawing-room or reception-room,
and as we had it all to ourſelves we were no
ſooner ſeated in our reſpective *bergères* at each
ſide of the bright crackling pine fire, than I was
determined to lead up to the matter that was
preoccupying me; and after having broached the
ſubject of apparitions in general, and individual
viſitations in particular, I aſked her point-blank
if ſhe believed in ſuch things?

" *Comment! ſi j'y crois? Eh! mon Dieu! nous
en ſavons bien aſſez!* " was her reply, with a mo-
mentary ſhudder.

I then ventured ſo far as to ſay, that the *on dit*
at —— was, that her ſiſter had once ſeen a viſion
of ſome ſort.

She ſhook her head two or three times, ſlowly
but affirmatively. At length ſhe ſaid, after a ſhort
pauſe—

" *Ecoutez!* I believe Stéphanie likes you well
enough to tell you the hiſtory herſelf, and to-night,

when everyone is gone, I will try and get her to do fo, and alfo to *fhow* you the proof of what fhe afferts. *Mais chut! la voici!"*

And as fhe fpoke *la veuve* entered, and as foon after, the guefts began to arrive, of courfe the converfation became general. But I refolved within myfelf that I wouldn't "go home till morning," if it were neceffary, in order to hear the ghoft ftory; in which expectation, I confefs, the evening appeared unufually long, notwithftanding that I had the good fortune to win an *étui*, with a gold thimble, fciffors, and needles, --moft ufeful things in themfelves, but to *me* rather in the category of what the failors call " a watch-pocket for a cow." However, no matter how agreeable or how ftupid a party may be, the time at length arrives when the comers muft go. And go they did—all but myfelf. I was the laft. I made a feint to follow the others, but Mélanie, propofing that "we three" fhould have a *bonne cauferie* and fome fpiced wine, I, with a faint fhow of refiftance, yielded to her *douce violence.*

" *Allons,"* faid fhe, *"racontez-nous, une de vos bonnes hiftoires."*

I obeyed with the moft amiable alacrity, and foon had both the fifters in fits of laughter. Mélanie then gave us an *impayable* anecdote of Madame de Staël-Holftein, which, though it

did very well *en petit comité*, as *she* managed to
tell it, would not exactly do for print, for we are
very proper in *print*—we Englifh, (would to
goodnefs we were equally fo in practice!). At
length it became the turn of Stéphanie to cater
for our amufement. She began by excufing her-
felf, faying fhe was fo ftupid that fhe really knew
nothing worth our liftening to.

"*Oh, que fi!*" protefted Mélanie; and rifing
and whifpering fomething in her fifter's ear, fhe
added aloud, "*Oui, de grâce, ma bonne Stéphanie,
je t'en prie!*"

And I adding my entreaties to hers, we at
length prevailed upon her to narrate the following moft extraordinary circumftance:

"I muft tell you that about fixteen years ago,
I was engaged to be married to M. Vanderveldt
de Witt, of Amfterdam. Everything was arranged for the wedding to take place in a month,
not in Holland but in Hungary, at the *château*
of my friend, the Comteffe de G——, whom
you have met here, and with whom I was then
ftaying on a vifit. It was late in October. I had
on the morning of the 23rd received an *écrin*
of very beautiful pearls and fapphires from my
fiancé, and very kind letters from his mother and
his fifter Madame G—— de Z——. We were
all in high fpirits, and at fupper (for in Hungary
and Germany in thofe days people fupped) the

Comte de G—— drank to the health of the future
bride and bridegroom. A withered old diplomate,
Baron von S——, alone refufed to drink the
toaft, faying it was unlucky, and quoting the
proverb, 'Many a flip 'tween the cup and the
lip.' As you may fuppofe, I thought this both
unkind and ill-bred, and left the table in tears.
Madame de G—— followed me up to my room,
abufing Baron von S——, who fhe faid had
always been an old *brouillon*, even in diplomacy,
which only required head and no heart, and
afked me how I could be fo filly as to let the
croaking of fuch a notorious old raven diftrefs
me, when I had had fuch cheering and delightful
letters that very morning, and would in one
little month be able triumphantly to refute the
Baron's bearifh growls? I replied, 'Ah! what
may not happen in or long before the expiration
of a month, and I be none the wifer?'[1]

   "' *Bah! eft elle donc bête, cette petite fiancée?*'
was her only anfwer, and fhe rang for Theckla,
my *femme de chambre*, and tapping me on the
cheek wifhed me good night. Now I muft tell
you that my bedroom was large and gloomy, an
old wainfcoted room, with the bed in an alcove,

---

[1] There were neither railways nor electric telegraphs on
any part of the Continent at that time, fo tnat the tranfit of
letters and all other news was flow, but by no means fure.

as the beds in those old Hungarian *châteaux*
generally are ; a good fire blazed on the hearth,
but not a single thing in the shape of water, hot
or cold, in the room ; for at the *inner* side of the
alcove (in which the bed fitted as *closely* as a
bracelet in a case) was a door opening into the
dressing-room, where there was another fire, with
a kettle of hot water, and all the hip-baths,
basins, cans of cold water, and other washing-
things ; so that had I wanted a glass of water, or
sirop, or *tisanne*, or anything, in the night, I must
either have got out of bed and gone into the
dressing-room for it, which was easy, the door
opening from the wall, inside the bed, or have
rung for it ; as, to save my life, I could not at
either side of the bed have had a table or chair,
however small, placed so as to have had a cup or
glass standing upon it.   You will see as I go on,
that it was necessary fully to explain this to you.
There was also of course *another* door into the
dressing-room at the end of the room, *outside* the
foot of the bed.   After I had washed and said
my prayers, Theckla stayed as usual to put out
the candles, both in the bedroom and dressing-
room, and then left me.   Tired out with the
excitement of the day, as well pleasurable as
painful, I fell asleep, and may have slept for
about an hour and a half, when I awoke with a
loud scream, having dreamt that I saw Carle de

Witt fall into some deep black-looking water, that I had caught hold of him to try and save him, but his coat had given way, and he fell in with a terrific splash! and that was it, that woke me; but imagine my horror when, as if to prove it was a reality and no dream, I felt all the front of my nightgown, from the ankles to the shoulders, wringing wet and deadly cold! I rang the bell at the head of the bed violently, for I was so paralyzed between grief and fear that I could not get out of bed. Theckla appeared, as soon as she could get down out of her own room, with a shawl hastily thrown over her shoulders and her stockingless feet thrust into her slippers.

"' *Mon Dieu! est-ce que mademoiselle est malade?*' said she, hurrying to the bedside with the light.

"'For heaven's sake, Theckla, look here! What *can* this be?' said I, putting my hand upon her shoulder and getting out of bed; when both she and I, to our terror and astonishment, beheld my night things, not only splashed with a black muddy water from the ankles to the shoulders, but *dripping wet*.

"' *Seigneur Dieu!*' she exclaimed, 'what has happened to you?"

"I first told her to bring me another nightgown, and on *no* account to have the one I took off washed, but to let it dry, and put it carefully by.

I then told her my dream. She was so aghast
that she made no attempt at refuting it, but kept
on wringing her hands and turning up her eyes.
I could not return to bed again, neither could
I stand. I made Theckla bring pen, ink, and
paper; I asked her to look at my watch and tell
me exactly what o'clock it was; and allowing for
the ten minutes that had elapsed from the time
I had rang my bell to the time it had taken her
to reach my room, and also allowing for the five
additional minutes it had taken me to tell her
my dream, I told her to write down in clear,
large, legible letters (for my own hand trembled
so much that I could not,) what I should dictate
to her, and then to pin the statement to the nightgown and put them both carefully away. She
accordingly wrote as follows, accompanying her-
self the while with innumerable "*Eh mon pères!*"
and "*Est-il possibles!*"

"'On the night of the 23rd of October, 18—,
Stéphanie de A— being at the *château* of the
Comte de G— in Hungary, near ——, dreamt,
at a quarter to twelve at night, that she saw
M. Carle Vanderveldt de Witt's foot slip, and
that he fell into some deep, black-looking water,
nd athat she in vain tried to save him, when she
awoke with the fright, and, wonderful to relate,
found the front of her nightgown wringing wet,
and splashed in a spiral and perpendicular direc-

tion, exactly as would have been the caſe had ſhe been ſtanding in it on the bank of a river and a heavy ſubſtance had fallen ſuddenly into the water.

" ' Witneſſed by me, THECKLA MORGANSTEIN,
at the Château de G——,
in Hungary, this night of the
23rd of October, 18—,
at half-paſt 12 at night.'

" I could not, as I have before ſaid," continued Stéphanie, " return to bed the whole of that night, and the next morning I was in a brain fever ; but as ſoon as letters could arrive from Holland, there came one to Madame de G—— from Marie de Witt (Madame G—— de Z——), to beg of her to break the fatal tidings to me. This letter bore the date of the 24th of October, and ſtated that on the previous day her brother Carle, had dined with her, and ſtayed late, talking over his future proſpects and approaching marriage. As the night was very foggy, ſhe wanted him to return home in her carriage, but he ſaid he preferred walking. Paſſing one of the canals, the fog became ſo denſe he could not ſee his hand before him, and ſtopping, it is ſuppoſed, to count the chimes of the Stadt Houſe clock, then ſtriking a quarter paſt twelve (at which hour his own watch was found to have ſtopped), on reſuming his course, as is supposed by the man at the bridge, who heard the heavy splash, his foot slipped and he fell into the canal. Lanterns and flambeaux were immediately brought, but it was half-an-hour before the body could be found, and then it was quite dead.

"Seeing is believing," added Stéphanie, her voice almost inarticulate with emotion, as she rose, and taking a small trefoil key out of her pocket, opened a drawer of an old carved oak *babut*, or cabinet, and produced the nightgown, with the paper Theckla had written still pinned to it. The dark splashes of foul, muddy water, exactly as she had described, broad and heavy at the skirt from the hem, and tapering and sprinkling in miry drops as the splash descended, was, without exception (under the circumstances), the most extraordinary thing I ever saw in my life. After we had all three gazed on it for full five minutes in profound silence, she took it, replaced it in the cabinet, put the key again in her pocket, and walked, without uttering a word, like a person in her sleep, out of the room.

"*Pauvre Stéphanie!*" murmured her sister.

"*Pauvre femme!*" sighed I, as I pressed Mélanie's hand, and quitted the house without any other adieux, to ponder on this strange, but ower true tale.

Before I narrate the other ghost story, which

was really an *apparition*, though in broad daylight, I may as well cite a few of Mr. Moreton's theories respecting apparitions. After largely quoting from what he is good enough to call " Mr. Milton's fine poem," he next proceeds to turn the greater part of the " Paradise Loft" into somewhat ludicrous profe, defcriptive of the Devil's innumerable metamorphofes to tempt Eve ; he then goes on through all his (Satan's) various apparitions, as well as the celeftial ones, throughout the Bible.

His claffification of fpirits is threefold; namely, angelic, or good ; demoniacal, or evil ; and the fouls of living or dead men, which are not neceffarily either evil or good, but from being *fpirit* and not matter, have perfect volition, and under peculiar and exceptional circumftances, and the will of a higher power, perfect ubiquity. And as an argument that our fpirits, or, as they are called in Scripture, our " angels," may appear to others, when our ftill living bodies are far diftant, he inftances Matthew xviii. 10, Chrift's faying of little children, " *in heaven their angels do always behold the face of My Father which is in heaven.*" And again, Acts xii. 15, when Peter knocked at the door where the difciples were gathered together, and they, believing him to be in chains and in the prifon, faid, " *It is his angel.*"

He then goes on to ſay, while theoriſing on the poſſible nature and attributes of ſpirits—

" Others run out to an imaginary ſcheme of guardian angels attending every man and woman while they are upon earth ; a notion ſo uncertain, if granted, and that has ſo many difficulties, that it is much better to leave it where it is, and which I ſhall explain preſently a much eaſier way.

" Now I ſay this is not my preſent buſineſs, to reconcile theſe diſtant and claſhing opinions, at leaſt not in this work. I have ſtarted a queſtion ; poſſibly my opinion is with the affirmative, at leaſt I think it poſſible, and that it is rational to believe it ; perhaps I may name you as improbable a notion, and much more inconſiſtent with the Chriſtian religion, which yet Philoſophy bids us call rational, and directs us to believe.

" How are we put to it, to form inhabitants for the planetary worlds ! Philoſophy ſays they are habitable bodies, ſolid, opaque, as the earth, and we will have them be inhabited alſo, whether it be with or without, for or againſt, our reaſon and underſtanding ; 'tis no ſatisfaction to them, or will it ſtop their cavils to ſay 'tis not a fact, that they are *not* habitable ; that both *Saturn* and *Jupiter* are uncomfortably dark, and inſufferably cold, and would congeal the very ſoul (if that were poffible), and fo are not habitable on that account. That *Mercury* and *Venus* are intolerably hot, that the very water would always boil, and the fire burn up the vitals, and that in fhort no human creatures could exift in fuch heat. But this is not fatisfactory neither, but rather than not have all thefe opaque worlds inhabited, and even their *Satellites*, or moons, about them too, they will have God be obliged to create a fpecies of bodies fuited to their feveral climates.

"In *Saturn* they are to live without eyes, or be as it were illuminated from their own internal heat and light, fo as that they can fee fuccinctly from their own beams.[1]

"In *Jupiter* there muft be another kind, who can live in twilight, and by the reflection of their own moons, and fubfift in a continued froft.[2]

"In *Mercury* the fpecies muft be all falamanders, and live in the continued fire of the fun's rays, more intenfe than what would be fufficient to burn all our houfes, and melt our iron, lead, and copper in the very mines. So that the inhabitants muft be of a kind better able to bear

---

[1] Even in our little homœopathic globule of a planet, the earth, many perfons do this, and many more would be far better off if they would do the fame. Only, unfortunately, thofe who are illuminated from within, with us—can't.

[2] Thefe *we* have alfo in perfection.

fire than thofe metals, and would ftill live, though they were continually calcining or vitrifying.

" In *Venus* the heat would boil the water, and confequently the blood in the body,[1] and a fet of human bodies muft be formed who could live always in a hot bath,[2] and neither fufe out their fouls nor melt their bodies.

" In *Mars*, fo very dry in its nature, no vegetables or fenfitives could fubfift that we have any notion of, for want of moifture ; and the men that lived there muft be dried up fufficiently for pulverization on any fuitable occafion,—I mean human beings of our fpecies.

" Now if God muft not be fuppofed to have created fo many habitable worlds without peopling them, and if it would reflect on his wifdom to lay fo much of His creation wafte that all the planets fhould feem to be made for nothing but to range about the wafte, as a kind of dark inhabitants, of no ufe but to fhine a little, and that with but borrowed luftre[3] too,

---

[1] In our little planet, the earth, it is juft the reverfe, for it is *ugly* things, more efpecially what is emphatically called " *an ugly bufinefs*," that makes *our* blood boil.

[2] Here we Earthmen fhow our fuperiority again ; for how many amongft us there are who *do* live continually in hot water, and by the *laws* of our planet, are never out of it !

[3] Here again we Earthites beat them hollow ; as we can, by innumerable modern inftances, prove that fuch a ftate of

upon this little point called earth, where only a ſet of rationals[1] can exiſt,—I ſay, if this muſt not be ſuppoſed; but on the contrary, that there are certainly people of one kind or another in all theſe worlds, let the trouble of making them be what it will; if this be the caſe, and if this muſt be believed in ſpite of many difficulties and inconſiſtencies, then allow me to argue a little upon the following inquiry :

"Why may I not as well ſuggeſt, and that with every jot as much probability, that there are, or at leaſt may be, a certain number of appointed inhabitants in the vaſtly extended abyſs of ſpace, a kind of ſpirits (other than the angels, good or bad, and alſo other than the unbodied or uncaſed ſouls of men,) who dwell in the inviſible world, and in the vaſt *nowhere* of unbounded ſpace, of which we can neither ſay what it is, what it contains, nor how determined? That great waſte, of the extent of which, it is hardly poſſible even the ſoul itſelf can conceive, and of which all the accounts we give and the gueſſes we make, are ſo remote, look ſo enthuſiaſtic, ſo improbable, and ſo like impoſſible, that inſtead of informing the ignorant part of the world by it, we only arm them with jeſt and ridicule, and

---

luminouſly uſeleſs exiſtence (or, at leaſt, of no uſe but to the owner), is quite poſſible.

[1] Query, irrationals ?

reſolve them in incurable unbelief, depending
that what it is not poſſible to conceive of is
not poſſible to be.

"Now is this immenſe ſpace indeed a void?
is it all a waſte? is it utterly deſolate? or is it
peopled by the Omnipotent Maker in a manner
ſuited to His own glory, and with ſuch inhabitants as are ſpiritual, inviſible, and therefore
perfectly proper to the place?

"I muſt needs ſay 'tis more rational to ſuggeſt
this to be, than to bring out a ſpecies of human
bodies to live in the intenſe heat of *Mercury* or the acute cold of *Jupiter* or *Saturn.*
The latter is agreeable to the general underſtanding we all have of ſpiritual[1] beings. We
are all well aſſured that there are ſome always
there, and that they can very well ſubſiſt there;
that the place is ſuitable to them, and that there
are ſpirits of ſome kind or other, and why not
ſuch as we ſuggeſt?

"It remains then only to examine what com-
munication theſe ſpirits have with us; whether
they are or are not able to hold converſation
with us, and whether they do converſe familiarly
with us, yea or no?"

---

[1] Or as Mr. Moreton calls them, "*ſpirituous*" beings;
So that one would really ſuppose that he was writing of the
denizens of our own little planet before the advent of
Father Mathew.

"If it ſhould be granted that there are ſuch ſpirits in exiſtence, and that they paſs and repaſs, live, and have egreſs and regreſs there: that they inhabit, as a certain bombaſtic author has it,

'Thro' all the liquid mazes of the ſky,'

I ſay, if this ſhould be granted, then it remains that there is a fourth ſpecies that may aſſume ſhapes; for ſpirits can do that, and may appear among us, may converſe with our embodied ſpirits, whether by dream, viſion, or apparition, or any ſuperior way, ſuch as to them, in their great knowledge of things, may ſeem meet. To ſpeak as diſtinctly of this nice point as I can, permit me to explain myſelf a little.

"If we grant that the ſpirit, though inviſible in itſelf, may aſſume ſhape, may veſt itſelf ſo with ſeeming fleſh and blood as to form an appearance, then all ſpirit may do it, ſince we have no rule given us by which we may diſtinguiſh ſpirits one from the other; I mean, as to their actings in the capacity of ſpirits. We may indeed, as I have ſaid already, diſtinguiſh them by the effect, that is to ſay, by the errand they come on, and by the manner of their operations; as whether they are good or evil ſpirits; but not by their nature *as* ſpirit.

"The devil is as really a ſpirit, though a degenerated, fallen, and evil ſpirit, I ſay he is as

much a ſpirit, to all the intents and purpoſes of
a ſpirit that we are capable of judging of, as an
angel   And he is called the Evil Spirit.   He
has inviſibility and multipreſence, as a ſpirit
has; he can appear, though the doors be ſhut,
and go out through them, though bolted and
barred.   No priſon can hold him, but his laſt
eternal dungeon.   No chain can bind him, but
the chains faſtened on him by heaven, and the
angel of the bottomleſs pit.   No engine or
human art can wound him.   In ſhort, he is
neither to be ſeen, felt, heard, or underſtood,
unleſs he pleaſes; and he can make himſelf be
both ſeen and heard too if he pleaſes; for he
can aſſume the ſhape of man or beaſt, and in
theſe ſhapes or appearances can make himſelf
viſible to us, terrify and affright us, converſe in
a friendly or a frightful manner with us, as he
thinks fit.   He can be a companion or a fellow-
traveller in the day, an apparition or a horrible
monſter in the night.   In a word, he can be
among us, and act upon and with us, viſibly or
inviſibly, as he pleaſes, and as he finds to his
purpoſe."

*   *   *   *   *

After reiterating this argument much in the
ſame ſtrain, the author again cites the apparitions
in ſacred hiſtory, pointing out and expatiating
upon the grandeur or neceſſity of theſe angelic

manifeſtations, and then adds, with much truth and ſome humour, with reſpeƈt to the general run of vulgar ſuperſtitions and popular errors and fallacies—'But here you have an old woman dead, one it may be that has hid a little money in the orchard or garden, and an apparition is ſuppoſed to come and diſcover it, by leading the perſon it appears to to the place, and makes a ſignal that he ſhould dig there. Or a man is dead, and having left a legacy to ſo-and-ſo, the executor does not pay it, and then an apparition comes, and haunts this fraudulent executor till he does juſtice and pays it. Is it likely an angel ſhould be ſent from heaven to find out the old woman's earthen diſh, with thirty or forty ſhillings in it? Or that an angel ſhould be ſent to haraſs this man for a legacy of perhaps five or ten pounds? And as to the *Devil*, will any one charge *him* with being ſolicitous to have juſtice done? Thoſe who know him at all muſt know him better than to think ſo erroneouſly of him.''

Another of his theories about the inviſible world is, that ſpirits are perhaps allowed to forewarn us of both coming good or evil and hence what we call "preſentiments;" but that they are not allowed to do more, that is, that they have no power to lead us aƈtually out of evil or into good. At this rate, what would be the uſe

of their myftical tale-bearing? And then again,
what "mocking devils" fome of thefe fpirits
muft be,

> " Who never warn us till the deed is done !"

Mr. Moreton then waxes warm, grows fatirical,
touching the fops of his own times, and grows
perfectly favage refpecting the ancient and honourable order of "free and accepted Mafons."
As I never belonged to the former, the ftill more
ancient, though lefs worfhipful order of Fops, I
fhall certainly not tarry to break lances for them ;
and as for the Freemafons, their order has fur-
vived all the quoits hurled at it by the malignant
Moreton, and their good deeds and Chriftian
philanthropy as men are the beft and moft
triumphant refutation of all calumnies againft
them, paft, prefent, or future. However,

> " Odiofa eft oratio, cum rem agas longinquum loqui ;"

So without any further beating about the bufh
or digreffion, I will juft give one more extract
from Andrew Moreton, as a curiofity of literature, and then proceed to "put in an appearance," *alias,* narrate my fecond ghoft ftory.

"This hypothefis of a fuppofed new clafs of
fpirits," fays Moreton, "would lead me into a
great many ufeful fpeculations ; and I might remark, with great advantages from it, upon the
general indolence which it is evident has fo fatally

poſſeſſed our men of wit in this age. To ſee a fool, a fop, believe himſelf inſpired! A fellow that waſhes his hands fifty times a day; but if he would be truly cleanly ſhould have his brains taken out and waſhed, his ſkull trepanned, and placed with the hind ſide before, that his underſtanding, which Nature placed by miſtake with the bottom upwards, may be ſet right, and his memory placed in a right poſition. To *this* unſcrewed engine talk of ſpirits and of the inviſible world, and of *his* converſing with unembodied ſoul, when he has hardly brains to converſe with anything but a barber or a powder puff, and owes it only to his being a fool that he does *not* converſe with the *Devil,* who, *if* he has any ſpirit about him, it muſt be one of thoſe indolent angels I ſpeak of; and if he has not been lifted among the infernals it has not been for want of wickedneſs, but only for want of wit.

" I DON'T wonder ſuch as thoſe go a mobbing among thoſe meaneſt of mad things called *Free-Maſons;* rough cheats and confeſſed deluſions are the fitteſt things to amuſe them. They are like thoſe fooliſh fiſh that are caught in large nets, that *might* get out at every ſquare meſh, but hang by the gills upon a mere thread, and chooſe to hamper and tangle themſelves when there is no occaſion for it, ſo that they are taken even in thoſe ſnares that are not laid for them.

" I now come to the main and moſt diſputed point of ſhadowy appearance, viz., the apparition of unembodied ſoul.

" It is a material difficulty here, and ought to be conſidered with the utmoſt plainneſs, viz., what we mean by *unbodied ſouls;* whether we underſtand by it ſouls which *have* been incaſed in fleſh, but being unhouſed are now moving about—in what ſtate we know not—and are to be ſpoken of in their ſeparate capacity; or whether there is any ſuch thing as A MASS OF SOUL, as a learned but inconſiſtent writer calls it, which is waiting to be embodied, as the ſuperior diſpoſer of that affair (be that who or what he pleaſes) may direct.

" This, I confeſs, is to me ſomething unintelligible, looks a little *Platonic,* and as if it were akin to the tranſmigration whimſey of the antients; but if they would found it upon anything rational, it muſt be on the ſuggeſtion mentioned above, viz. of a middle claſs of ſpirits, neither angelic-heavenly nor angelic-infernal, but ſpirits inhabiting the inviſible ſpaces, and allowed to act and appear here under expreſs and greatly ſtrained limitations, ſuch as are already deſcribed, and of which much more may ſtill be ſaid.

" But that I may clear up your doubt as to the point I am upon, I have added at the head of this ſection the word '*Departed,*' to intimate to

you that I am orthodox in my notion, and that
I am none of the fect of foul-fleepers, or for im-
prifoning fouls in the *Limbus* of the antients ; but
that in a few words, by the appearance of fouls
unembodied, I mean fuch as, having been embodied or imprifoned in flefh, are difcharged from
that confinement, or, as I call it, unhoufed, and
turned out of poffeffion; for I cannot agree that
the foul is in the body as in a prifon, but rather
that, like a rich nobleman,[1] he [I thought the
foul was feminine?] is pleafed to inhabit a palace
of his own building [!] where he refolves to live
and enjoy himfelf, and does fo, till by the fate of
things, his fine palace being overturned, whether
by earthquake or otherwife, is buried in its own
ruins, and its noble owner turned out of poffeffion without a houfe.

    " This foul, we are told (and I concur in the
opinion), has fometimes made a tour back into
this world, whether earth, or the atmofphere of
the earth—call it what you will, and exprefs it
how you will, it matters not much. Whence it
comes, how far the journey, how and why it came
hither, and above all, how it goes back again,
and what thofe various apparitions are which

---

[1] Then how about thofe fouls incarcerated in the fuffering,
ftruggling, ftarving bodies of poor beggars, and in thofe of (the
worft fort of paupers) poor gentlemen and gentlewomen?

counterfeit theſe ſpirits,—enquire within, and you
ſhall know farther.

"That the unembodied ſouls of dead men, or
as we ſay, departed, *have* appeared, we have
affirmed from the authority of Scripture, which I
muſt allow to be an authentic document, whatever
the reader may pleaſe to do, till a hiſtory more
authentic and of better authority may be produced in the room of it."

In ſhort, Mr. Moreton goes on to prove, by
many marvellous, well-authenticated hiſtories,
that as we ſhould put on our cloaks or great
coats for an airing, ſo diſembodied ſpirits ſome-
times put on their bodies, or body coats, for a
ſtroll back into this world, which, if they were
wiſe ſouls, they would be only too glad to get out
of, and be well rid of that cumbrous natural
crinoline, the body. Though truly, the following hiſtory goes far to confirm Mr. Moreton's
theory.

As I before premiſed, the chief actor in this
moſt extraordinary apparition ſtory was by no
means an imaginative, or even an impreſſionable
perſon, nor yet a *raconteur;* he was ſimply a
highly reſpectable paterfamilias, of ſtrict probity and ſcrupulous veracity, of middle age, and
rather taciturn, when I knew him, or, it might be,
ſobered by that moral ſoda-water, the cares of a
large family, and that moſt ſedative of all fever

draughts, high birth and low means. He had formerly been in a crack cavalry regiment, and winced, *tant soit peu*, as Mr. Moreton's "*great noblemen souls*" are apt to do when thrust into a hovel instead of a palace of flesh ; in fact, he did not like—who does ?—the change from the brocade to the huckaback of life ; but he so far bowed to the rod as to take to it, and was so inveterate an angler and so keen a sportsman that there was no distance too great for him to go, nor no trouble too much for him to take, for the chance of a bite ; he haunted every stream, and therefore knew the favourite haunts of every trout and grayling for miles round. I can well understand how either the meditative or the miserable, are so fond of angling, were it only for the blessed practical wisdom of the angler's motto—"I watch and I hope." But what I *don't* understand is, how, from being planted so long in the damp grass, with a watery grave before them, and little fishes eternally popping up their heads open-mouthed against them, like those in the enchanted frying-pan of the Arabian Nights—what I cannot understand, I say, is, that they don't get a chronic pursed-up mouth *en cœur*, like that of their patron saint, dear old Izaac Walton himself, as he has come *flâneur*-ing down to posterity in that prim perch of a looking portrait that hangs out like a sign

at the frontispiece of his lives of Donne, Hooker,
Sir Henry Wotton, George Herbert, &c., and
where it is as palpable and patent, as if his wife
had just whispered the fact to one, and that one
smelt the lavender out of the drawer from which
they had been taken—that that rigidly new
doeskin glove and those two broad, massive, fine
gold rings were not put on *every* day!—and a
good thing too, for as Mr. Fact used to observe
in Charles Matthews senior's inimitable *répertoire*,
they'd "*frighten the fish!*" No, I'm not sur-
prised at men whom that jade, Fortune, has
jilted becoming anglers, for if they can but
keep their fancies from vagabondising after
"Shelsey cockles," "Chichester lobsters," "Arun-
del mullet," and "Amerly trout," what a dual
lesson of patience under disappointment, and
habits of strict temperance may the Fordidge
trout teach them! which saith Walton—"never
afford an angler any sport, but either live their
time of being in the fresh water by their
meat formerly gotten in the sea, (not unlike
the swallow or frog), or by the virtue of the
fresh water only, or as the birds of paradise
and the chameleons are said to live, by the sun
and the air;"—which, as any parish beadle or
overseer, or even aristocratic philanthropist, can
tell you, is precisely the proper diet and allowance for poor, and more especially for destitute,

bipeds. Then, none but those who have tried
it, know the soothing mysteries of ivy-juice;
which, while it bewitches the fish, "cheers and
not inebriates" the gentleman by whom, poor
silly thing, she is so taken. But even the
oldest angler in the world, HOPE! not only
ceases to angle, but ceases to exist, when she
is quite sure that the waters are so troubled
that she can catch nothing, various as her baits
are : for ambition, power ; for avarice, wealth ;
for love, phantom hearts, that in his own sun-
light *look* like golden ones, wreathed with chains
of everlasting flowers, which do admirably to
strew upon his own early grave ; for poverty,
guineas; and for indefatigable anglers, guiniads.
Ah! whether we look down into the stream,
which, like our life, is ever flowing from us,
or up, into the heavens, which are eternally
awaiting us—

> Hopes, what are ye? April showers,
> A rainbow, for life's waiting hours;
> Bright tints that span far distant spheres,
> All fading as that future nears!

Yet, sweetest and gentlest of all spirits, visible
or invisible, sister of charity of the heart, minis-
tering angel of the mind—who ever dwellest with
the poor and lowly, and bindest up the gaping
wounds made by cruelty and injustice ; who when
we faint and writhe on earth whisperest of Heaven;

who, when caſt away and tempeſt-toſt, faveſt us
with thine anchor—think not that for worlds of
realized happineſs I would be ſo impious as to
breathe one diſparaging word of thee ! For when
at laſt thou leaveſt us, it is but in the ſpirit of
truth, becauſe thou knoweſt that when Fate has
left nothing to thee, there is no longer anything
for us, and thou muſt of neceſſity give up thy
garriſon ; for when a life has been poiſoned, not
only at every fource, but through every channel,
thou, with all thy bleſſed healing art, canſt only
for a time mitigate ſuffering ; thou canſt not give
an effectual antidote ; Death alone can do that.
But ſo good, ſo kind, art thou, that the poor
four-footed creatures thou leadeſt with a furer
inſtinct than ourſelves, or elſe never would the
poor Vicar have exclaimed, in (the moſt touching
of all the records of one of God's ready-made
angels) his journal :[1]

"Truly, there muſt be ſomething which attracts
the unfortunate towards me ; if anyone is in want
he comes firſt to me—me ! who have ſo little to
give. I have remarked alſo, that when I am
dining anywhere from home, and there is a dog
in the houſe, it is on my knee that he always lays
his cold noſe firſt in ſearch of a morſel."

---

[1] One of the moſt, not to ſay the moſt, charming ſtories
ever written, " Journal of a Poor Vicar," by Henry Zſchokke.

But I ſee Colonel H. has got his baſket and all his fiſhing-tackle ready, and as to his varieties of bait, I rejoice that I am neither angler nor natu-raliſt enough to deſcribe them ; no doubt *he* had read every line of Ulyſſes Aldrovandus "De Piſcibus;" I have not, and I'll venture to ſay *you* have not either, Reader, which will give us the leſs to carry, ſo let us ſet out. There is no uſe in telling the world at large (which, I dareſay, has other fiſh to fry,) how in the brawling, bubbling, bounding Dee, Colonel H. broke one rod with a crafty old barbel. For, as Walton affirmeth, "the barbel affords the angler choice ſport, being a luſty and a cunning fiſh ; ſo luſty and cunning as to endanger the breaking of the angler's line by running his head forcibly towards any covert or hole in the bank, and then ſtriking at the line, to break it off with his tail; as is obſerved by Plutarch in his 'De Induſtriâ Animalium ;' and alſo ſo cunning as to nibble off your worm cloſe to the hook, and yet avoid letting the hook come into his own mouth."

Bullied by this diplomatic old barbel, deter-mined to walk much further on towards a moun-tain (for it was in North Wales), to a quieter part of the river, where he knew the trout moſt did congregate, at length he walked ſo far, that he quite loſt his way ; but having had excellent ſport during the day, he had not, till the ſun

began to ſink into its gorgeous bed of crimſon
and gold, remarked how far he had ſtrayed out
of his uſual beat. He began to look about him in
queſt of a road one way or the other, but above
him was nothing but mountains, behind him in-
terminable thickets of underwood and ſtunted
oak, and before him the ſhallow river, where no
coricle could have ſkimmed, on account of the
giant ſtones ſcattered in all directions and riſing
from the bed of the river, always ſhallow at this
juncture in ſummer : ſo ſhallow, that anyone as
nimble as Colonel H. was might with eaſe have
croſſed it by jumping from ſtone to ſtone, without ever wetting his feet. It however never
entered his head juſt at that time to think of croſſing it ; he was ravenouſly hungry—completely
déſorienté, not to ſay *déſarçonné*—and not a human
being of whom, or even a human habitation where,
he could have aſked his way ; no, nor even an
intelligent ſheep-dog, that can do better than
ſpeak—for they always act, and that ſenſibly
and effectually. The landſcape was ſtill flooded
with the glorious light of the departing ſun,
but ſtill, above his golden diadem was one of
thoſe draperies of purple-black clouds which in
mountainous countries are the ſure heralds of
a coming and ſudden ſtorm.

"Well, this is pleaſant !" ſaid Colonel H.,
looking about him in all directions for at leaſt

the twentieth time. " What on earth am I to
do ? I fee no road in any direction ; and to go
back, dodging along the river as I came, at this
hour and a ftorm coming on, would be madnefs."
And again he afked himfelf out loud what he
was to do, without obtaining any more fatisfactory anfwer. Then adding in his own mind, " I
wonder, if I croffed over to the other fide, whether
I fhould find any fort of a road?" In order to
do fo, he ftooped down to pick up fome of his
fifhing tackle, and arrange it more compactly and
portably on the top of his bafket. As he looked
up from completing his packing he faw, ftanding
oppofite to him, on one of the large ftones in the
centre of the bed of the river, an exceedingly ·
pretty little girl between five and fix years old,
with dark blue eyes, bright golden hair, that fell
from under a large round ftraw hat in a profufion
of ringlets on her fhoulders. She had on a little
dark blue or purple bodice, with a bright red
petticoat, little white focks, with black fhoes buttoned round the ankle, with a ftrap from the
heel, fuch as young children wear. But as fhe
ftood, the fun forming a complete halo round her,
fhe looked far more like a little opera *coryphée*
than a peafant's child.

After having gazed at her for about a fecond
in furprife and admiration, Colonel H. called
out—

"Ho! I ſay, my pretty little girl! can you tell me if there is any road or houſe near this? There muſt be ſome houſe, or elſe you would not be here."

No anſwer. The child moved on, *how*, he could not tell, as ſhe certainly neither jumped nor made any other movement; ſtill, ſhe had advanced three or four ſtones further on, but kept looking back at him, not with what is generally denominated a ſmile, but ſomething more; it appeared like an irradiation from within, lighting up her whole face, without however any muſcular movement of the mouth or any other feature.

"'Pon my word," ſaid he, "you are a pretty, fantaſtic little creature! not a common child, evidently. I wonder who you are, and how they came to let you out by yourſelf, to take ſuch a dangerous ramble!"

And then he repeated his former queſtion in a louder voice.

Still no anſwer, but the child kept looking wiſtfully back at him.

"Do you mean that I ſhould follow you?" he aſked. She ſlightly nodded her head.

"Well, by Jove, I *will!*" cried he, jumping at once from ſtone to ſtone into the centre of the river, and trying to balance himſelf like a man on a tight-rope without a balancing pole. But by the time he had reached the ſecond large ſtone, where the child had ftood, fhe was again feveral yards in advance of him.

"Come, tell me your name, there's a good little girl?"

But fhe only accelerated her pace—*how*, he could not tell, as, watch as clofely as he would, or, rather, as he could, in the attention he was obliged to beftow on his own ftepping, he could not difcover; but upon looking fuddenly up after one of his own tranfits, he perceived fhe was then at a confiderable diftance from him.

"Heyday! my dear little Will-o'-the-wifp! this will never do. I really cannot get over the ground, or rather, over the ftones, as you do."

The child paufed, and remained perfectly motionlefs for about five minutes, till he had come up with her, to within a few yards, when he ftretched out his hand, refolved to clutch her drefs, that fhe fhould not again efcape him; but he only clutched the air, and fhe was once more ever fo far before him. And then again fhe ftood quite ftill, to give him time to reach her; but, as before, in vain he tried to touch her, for in an inftant fhe was yards further.

In fhort, this fort of phantom chafe continued for more than an hour, and extended over full three miles, the clouds gradually growing darker and more portentous, till at length a loud clap of thunder, accompanied by a vivid flafh of light-

ning and a few large heavy drops, announced
that the gathering ftorm had culminated. Colonel
H. was beginning to experience a degree of
myftification that almoft amounted to fear, as he
recalled all the wild legends of the Hartz and the
Lurlei, and did not half relifh the idea of *his*
being felected as Goblin Mafter of the Revels, to
take the initiative in introducing them into England, or at leaft Wales, which was much the fame
thing. So fuddenly ftopping, he called out at the
top of his voice—

" I tell you what, my little fprite—elf, fairy,
or whatever you are! I'm not going to be led
this wildgoofe chafe by you all night; fo if you
won't tell me your name, or at leaft where you
are going and what you want, I'll turn back,—
which I was a precious fool not to have done
long ago."

The child again ftood perfectly ftill, and looked
back at him. She did not beckon, neither did fhe
fold her hands and hold them up, as if praying;
but deep as the twilight now was, he could fee
the expreffion of her face as clearly as if it had
been noon; her very foul feemed, as it were, to
be kneeling in her eyes, and faid more im-
ploringly than any words could have done—

" Do, *pray do,* come on!" And in fpite of
himfelf, and without any volition in the matter,
on he went, for it might be about another mile;

it was now quite dark, the rain falling in torrents, but his myſterious little leader was occaſionally revealed to him by a vivid flaſh of lightning. He by this time felt that ſort of reckleſs reſolution which may be termed the courage of deſpair, and he would not have turned back if he could; and ſtrange to ſay, now that he had ceaſed to ſee where he was going, and therefore carefully to pick his ſteps, he ſeemed to bound on with a ſort of involuntary and preternatural elaſticity. At length there came one broad vivid flaſh, that ſteeped the whole landſcape in flame for about a ſecond, and revealed to him, on the right-hand ſide of the river, a thickly-wooded mountain ſide, with a ſteep narrow ſheepwalk winding-up it. Thither the child now darted, as uſual, firſt looking back at Colonel H. to follow,—a mandate which he had no longer either the power or the inclination to reſiſt; and he even experienced a ſort of phyſical relief at finding himſelf once more on *terra firma.* The rain by this time was coming down in ſuch rivulets, that it made that hiſſing, ſeething ſort of noiſe, which reſembles the ſhooting of cart-loads of gravel; and after about half-an-hour's more walking, or rather being propelled by ſome unaccountable impetus, he ſuddenly ſtopped, breathleſs, panting, and drenched to the ſkin, when another flaſh of electric fluid, leſs vivid, but more blue and lurid than the one which had difclofed the fheep-walk at the foot of the mountain, now fhowed him a fmall cottage like a fhepherd's hut, againft the door of which, the little figure leant, and with a fmile that was perfectly feraphic, beckoned to him, pointed to the door, and as he ftretched out his hand to grafp hers immediately difappeared! For a few feconds Colonel H. remained breath-lefs and ftupefied, not well knowing whether his imagination had become the fport of fome fan-taftic dream, or whether he was really a waking fane man; at all events, the exhauftion, and the wet, with which his clothes were faturated, were but too real. After wringing fome of the water from his coat, he put out his hand in the direc-tion that a minute or two before, he had feen by the lightning was the cottage door, though half dreading that it would only again meet with empty air; but to his inexprefﬁble relief it met with the folid refiftance of an oaken door, upon which he loft no time in knocking loudly with his knuckles. No anfwer; or if there was one, the fierce loud conteft between the wind and rain prevented his hearing it. So he knocked again, louder than before, and called out, " Any one within? For the love of heaven open the door!" and before he had well ceafed fpeaking, a bolt was drawn, and the fharp click of an iron latch announced the opening of the door, at which an old woman, with one of thoſe dazzlingly white, well-ſtarched linen mob-caps that the Welſh peaſant women wear, and a grey plaid ſhawl over that again, (as a protection againſt the ſtorm,) appeared on the threſhold, and ſaid in Welſh, and in the uſual national high, ſhrill, quick key, " Is that you, Amos Price ? it 's time for you, leaving me all theſe hours with what can never be company to me again, poor dead lamb ! poor dead lamb ! We had no buſineſs to make a king's child of her, as we did, and ſo God has taken her, as we made an angel of her."

The concluſion of this ſpeech was ſobbed out rather than ſpoken, and Colonel H., not waiting for an invitation, walked in, ſlammed to the door, and ſaid to the old woman, in as much Welſh as he could muſter, that he was not Amos Price, but an Engliſh gentleman, who had loſt his way in the mountains, and that if ſhe would allow him to dry his clothes, paſs the night on the oak bench beſide her fire, and dreſs him ſome trout for his ſupper (of which he had brought plenty) he would pay her well for her trouble.

The latter ſentence is one that never fails to be heard by the deafeſt Welſh ears and to touch even the hardeſt Welſh heart. So the old woman dropped a low curtſey, with a—

" Yes, ſure, ſir !" adding, " Eh ! but *hur's* juſt *arownded !*" in her beſt Engliſh, proceeding to

difencumber her unexpected gueſt of his coat
and fiſhing-rods; after which ſhe knelt down
before the wood embers burning on the hearth,
and blowing them with her breath, lit a ruſh-
light, and from it, to do all honour to her viſitor,
a ſmall lamp in a tin ſconce, that hung above one
of the oak ſettles inſide the ponderous chimney;
while a wooden ſcreen of nearly black oak, di-
vided into ſquare compartments, like a window
frame, and poliſhed by time, projected from the
right-hand ſide of the fireplace, to keep off the
draught from the door and the window, as is
common in old Welſh farm-houſes and cottages.
Meanwhile, Colonel H. took off his hat and
coat, and aſked the old woman to hang the latter
on the back of a chair to dry; while ſhe, perceiving by the light that he really was a gentleman, redoubled in her alacrity and civility, and
while, according to his directions, ſhe was taking
the fiſh out of the baſket, ſaid—

"I'm ſure I beg *hur* pardon, but I thought te
was my old man come back."

And here ſhe put the corner of her apron to
her eyes and ſighed deeply.

Colonel H., pre-occupied with his ſtrange
adventure, flung himſelf into the oak ſettle inſide
the warm old chimney corner, and ſtretching his
feet to the full length of it (firſt having taken off
his boots and put them to dry againſt one of the

iron dogs), while he gazed liſtleſſly at the fire for a few ſeconds, experienced that luxurious *dolce far niente* which a reclining poſition after extreme fatigue always ſuperinduces. Meanwhile, the old woman beſtirred herſelf, and laid a clean, coarſe, unbleached cloth on a little round table, with knife, fork, pepper, ſalt, and a brown loaf, and having put two plates againſt the other iron dog oppoſite the boots to get hot, reached down a fryingpan from among ſome bright tin ſaucepan covers, and a ſmall braſs peſtle and mortar that graced the mantlepiece. And it was not till Colonel H. heard the welcome ſounds of the trout being initiated into the habits of civilized life, that he was rouſed from his reverie, and half ſtarting up, ſaid—

"I'm ſure I'm very much obliged to you! I'm ſorry to give you ſo much trouble. Can I help you?"

"Ha, ha! *te* ain't no trouble; put hur ſorry hur ain't cot no pier, nor cider, nor nothing put water."

"Never mind," ſaid her gueſt, laughing, and rubbing his hands, as ſhe now transferred the trout to a hot diſh and placed it on the table; "Never mind, for my ſpeckled friends, here are all temperance people, and never touch anything elſe; but if you will be ſo good as to give me a glaſs of water, I'll drink your and their health, for I'm choking with thirſt."

After he had fulfilled his promiſe and pledged the old woman, H. bowed to the trout, and ſaid—

"Gentlemen, here's to you! I'm charmed to ſee you, but as *l'éloge ſe fait en mangeant*, I'll ſoon prove my ſincerity," and cutting a thick piece off the brown loaf, he ſoon began to eat, as men do eat, who have walked and faſted nearer twelve hours than ten. As ſoon as his hunger was in ſome degree appeaſed, *viâ* a ſecond *entrée* of the ſame diſh, he aſked the name of his preſent whereabout. The old woman told him ſome unpronounceable Welſh name, which got entangled in the burr in her throat and left him as wiſe as he was before. Fortunately, he was in the habit, on his fiſhing expeditions, of ſleeping at little village inns, ſo that his family, knowing how far his favourite paſtime led him, would not be alarmed at his abſence on the preſent occaſion; ſtill, being determined to return as early as poſſible in the morning, he now aſked his hoſteſs how far they were from ——? She told him fifteen miles.

"Whew!" ſaid he, giving a long whiſtle, deadly tired as he was that night, and having to paſs it without a bed, not much reliſhing the idea of ſo long a walk before breakfaſt. "I wonder," ſaid he, "you are not afraid to live in ſuch a lonely place."

"What would we have to be te feared of?

Poor people like us have no need to be te feared
te thieves."

" Well, I don't exactly mean thieves ; but
witches and ghoſts, and that ſort of thing."

" Eh ! te was only in old times there was ſuch
things as them ; there ain't none now."

" What? out of ſeaſon, eh ? like green peas at
Chriſtmas. So you have no faith in ſpirits ? "

" If my old man was te home he could get
hur *ſperits* at the ' Queen's Head,' but we ha'nt
none."

Colonel H. ſmiled, and aſſured her he
would not trouble her old man for any ſuch
purpoſe. He then ſaid, looking up at her bright
array over the mantlepiece, " You have a ſnug
little nook of it here, and you keep it very
nicely, which is the whole ſecret of making any
place nice or the reverſe, be it a palace or a
hovel."

And then he caſt a look all round. Oppoſite
to him was what he ſuppoſed to be a bed in a
receſs, by the blue and white checked curtains,
with plaited valance at the top that was
drawn before it. When, as his eyes travelled
round, and reſted on the wall oppoſite the large
fireplace, upon which an additional faggot now
made a cheerful blaze, his cheek blanched and
he gave a ſudden ſtart ; for there he ſaw hanging
up, *the* little red petticoat, blue bodice, and

large round ſtraw hat, that the phantom child
who had lured him to the cottage had worn!
while, that no ſingle identification might be
wanted, on a table underneath them, on the top
of a large Bible, were placed the little black kid
ſhoes and a pair of white ſocks.

"Good heavens!" ſaid he, addreſſing the old
woman, as he felt the cold drops of terror ſtanding on his forehead, while he pointed to them,
"To whom do thoſe little clothes belong?"

The old woman ſank down into a low chair,
and covering her face with her hands, and rock-
ing herſelf backwards and forwards, ſobbed
out—

"They did belong to our little Amy, but
ſhe'll never put them on again; ſhe's with the
angels now, and it's juſt to the Vicarage at ——
that Amos Price is gone, to tell the daughter of
the Vicarage [1] how it happened; and as ſhe was
ſo fond of the poor little ſoul, and taught her to
read, and all her pretty ways—too pretty, it ſeems,
for this world!—to ſee if ſhe could not get enough

---

[1] In North Wales the common people ſeldom give perſons
their proper name, but generally call them by that of the name
of the houſe, or even of the ſign of the public-houſe, where
they live; ſo that it is a common thing to hear a publican's
ſon deſignated by the Oſſianic and grandiloquent title of
"the Son of the Eagle," or his daughter, by the Oriental
one of "the Daughter of the Moon;" and it is always the
ſon or daughter "of the vicarage," and never "of the vicar."

from the gentlefolks, that uſed to be good to her, to put up a ſtone to her; for I ſhould be ſorry for her little grave to be loſt in nettles and weeds—ſhe that was ſo fond of flowers, and brought home ſuch a frockful from the mountain the very day before. But I've put 'em all ready for her to take with her. My old man ſaid it was nonſenſe, for there were better flowers in Heaven; but hur loved thoſe while hur was here, and hur *ſhall* have them." And here the poor old creature went off into a violent paroxyſm of hyſterics.

Colonel H. roſe and brought her a glaſs of water, and ſaid to her ſoothingly,—for indeed the tears were in his eyes, as he thought, although thoſe who had loved poor little Amy would never ſee her in her bright little fantaſtic dreſs again, how recently and ſtrangely he had done ſo; though there it hung, at once myſtifying, baffling, and confounding his reaſon, on that white wall before him,—yea, almoſt tenderly, he ſaid to her, for he ſpake from his heart—

"Don't fret yourſelf about a tombſtone for your little Amy; I'll take care that ſhe has one as pretty as herſelf."

"Cot pleſs hur! I'm ſure, ſir, I thank hur kindly. Ah, ſhe *was* pretty! You would have ſaid ſo, ſir, but you never ſaw her."

He did not care to contradict her, and ſo merely ſaid—

" Poor little thing, ſhe was your child ?"

" Grandchild, ſir."

And again the old woman covered her face, and rocked herſelf to and fro.

" Ah, I ſuppoſe her parents are away?" probed Colonel H., his curioſity excited to know how the very commonplace old peaſant woman before him could be really the grandmother of ſo beautiful and poetical looking a child.

" Parents, indeed !" muttered the old woman.

" What? ſhe hadn't any?   Both dead ?"

" Yes, yes ; ſhe had a mother, *my* child, worſe luck!   She was as pretty as Amy.   It's a great curſe, a great ſnare, ſir, is beauty !"

And here ſhe burſt into a freſh paroxyſm of tears.   Colonel H. perceived there was ſome painful hiatus in the child's parentage, and was at no loſs to fill it up.   So not additionally to diſtreſs the poor old woman by again alluding to this point, he merely ſaid—

" When did your poor little Amy die ?"

" Only yeſterday, ſir."

" Dear me, how ſad !   Was ſhe long ill ?"

" No, no !—*drownded, drownded !*"

And again ſhe rocked herſelf backwards and forwards, in uncontrollable grief.   At length ſhe ſaid, looking up at him—

" Do look at her, ſir ; it's not like death, it's juſt like a picter."

And taking the lamp from out of the chimney
ſhe walked to the bed and drew aſide the curtain, when to Colonel H.'s ineffable ſurpriſe,
and not without a cold ſhudder running through
his very marrow, he beheld—as if in that calm
and profound ſleep which only children know,
and which, from its peaceful beauty, angels may
well be ſuppoſed, not only to watch over, but to
whiſper every dream that haunts it—yes, there he
beheld the little figure that had ſo long flitted
before him and lured him to the cottage! the
rich maſſes of her ſilken hair ſhading her beautiful
face, and falling like ſhowers of rippling gold
againſt the marble of her cheeks and the ſnowy
whiteneſs of her little night-dreſs, while the little
hands were folded on her boſom ; and placed
under them, and ſupported by her cheſt, ſince the
muſcles that death had relaxed could no longer
hold them, was a bunch of faded wild flowers,
the very laſt, as the old woman informed him,
that ſhe had gathered the morning of her death,
a few hours before ſhe had fallen into the
river.

Colonel H. felt a choking, ſuffocating ſenſa-
tion in his throat and a moiſture in his eyes that
made him want to get into the air ; and yet, as
he honeſtly confeſſed to me, he did not like venturing to leave the cottage alone.

" Poor little Amy !" ſaid he, "you were indeed

beautiful! but you are better off now, for you are where you will never be lefs fo."

He gently drew the curtain, turned away from the bed, put a fovereign into the woman's hand, and afked her where fhe intended to have the child buried, for, as he before told her, he would take care fhe fhould have a fuitable monument, for which the old woman was profufe in her bleffings and thanks. He then afked her if there was no village near, where he could procure any fort of conveyance to return by that night. She faid, " Yes, at Llantys" fomething, where the Vicarage was fituated, which was only two miles from thence; and that when Amos Price returned he fhould fhow him the way.

So, defpite his impatience to be gone, as the ftorm had now ceafed and the moon was fhining brilliantly, he was fain to wait patiently for another hour, till the old man came back.

This ftrange ftory I tell as it was told to me. In the ftrict veracity of the chief actor in it, who narrated it to me, I have implicit faith, knowing it to be unimpeachable. As to explaining fuch things, that is beyond mortal ken; and though *cui bono*-ing them may prove our ignorance, it cannot enlighten it. But of this I am convinced, that our intelligence, when even of the moft exalted nature of which humanity is capable, is, by an all-wife Omnipotence, advifedly made finite; for if " by fearching we *could* find out," or by fpeculating we *could* foar to, and penetrate the myfteries of the infinite, not *one* of us, from the monarch who beftows honours, to the mendicant who begs alms, would or could, for even a fingle hour, go his circumfcribed and monotonous rounds in *the* particular mill allotted to each of us, and which, however apparently and compara- tively infignificant, is as *abfolutely* neceffary to the vaft machinery of God's concrete and complex creation as A WHOLE, and the progreffive work- ing out of its ultimate defign, as are the broad bafis, or the all-important axis, of

"THE GREAT GLOBE ITSELF."

And now, Reader, once more farewell ! This is an archæological and curiofity-feeking age. In the hope of amufing you through an idle hour, I have placed before you a few quaint old things from the Regalia of Remphan, which are not to be found even in the right good collection of the South Kenfington Mufeum. If they are not fortunate enough to pleafe you, the fault is not wholly mine, becaufe the matter is not wholly mine ; I have only been a bad purveyor, of which there are but too many in this utilitarian age. I can, therefore, but confcientioufly affure you that

I have adulterated none of the articles, but have given them to you genuine as I imported them.

Fabian, Speed, Stow, Sir Matthew Hale, Camden, and Bishop Fleetwood (the latter in his "Chronicon Preciosum"), all tell us that up to the reign of John both the bold barons and the monks were allowed to coin their own money [1] —delightful privilege! which they so abused that at length it was refcinded [2] (an abuse which perhaps in the prefent day fometimes extends to authors in the habit of coining their own books). So that this right, at length became vefted folely in the Crown, the confequence of which was, that each reign had a different coinage peculiar to itfelf. From the mancas of the Saxons, to the

---

[1] But even after they were deprived of this privilege the Crown occafionally, by various charters and grants, allowed feveral bifhoprics and abbeys the right to erect a mint within their own jurifdiction, and there to coin their own money ; fuch as the Abbot of St. Edmund's Bury, the Archbifhop of York, and the Bifhop of Durham. But they had not the domination of ftamp or alloy. Camden mentions having feen fome copper coinage of the time of Claudius Cæfar, ftruck in London, and bearing the infcription *Pecunia Londoni Signata*, and others when London was called Augufta, with that of *Præpofitus Thefaurorum Augustantium*, namely, "The treafurer of the mint of Augufta," or London.

[2] It was Henry II., not John, that put a ftop to this coining ufurpation of the baronage. He coined new money, and ordained that none other but what iffued from the royal mint fhould pafs current throughout his kingdom.

mark of the Middle Ages, the groffus or groat,[1] the filver penny, (firft weighed againft wheat grains), the Efterlings, as they were called, the *oboli* (galley-pence—fo called from being imported from Genoa, with which we had once great trade), the crocards or cocodines and rofaries (all afterwards called in by Elizabeth), the falutes or angels (ftruck in France by Henry V., and made current in England), the pollards, ftepings, ftaldings, fufkins, blanks of Henry VII., the dandypratts and the doitkins (alfo ftruck by Henry V., and from this latter comes our to this day current expreffion of " not worth a doit"), the deep, rough, indented croffed coin of the Conqueror, made fo deep as to be eafily broken in halves or quarters for purpofes of traffic, before halfpence and farthings were invented ; the gold halfpennies and farthings (!) of Edward III.[2] and

---

[1] In 1378 a groat, or 4*d.*, was paid to the king for every man and woman ;—a very pretty little poll-tax, and hence, no doubt, the origin of the faying, " Not worth a groat," which, poor creatures, it may be fuppofed one-half of them were not, either in a moral or monetary point of view.

[2] According to Fabian, Edward III. it was, who firft caufed farthings and halfpennies to be coined *round*, and as a feparate coin, for till then the croffed coin of William the Conqueror, had been broken into halves and quadrantes, or farthings ; and Fabian gives the following piece of " poetry " as he calls it, made at the time to commemorate the *royal* invention :—

Richard II., the angels, rose nobles, and spur
royals of Elizabeth and James I.'s times; the
Commonwealth crowns, with their Pharisaical
motto of "GOD WITH US;" yea verily! from
the first coin struck by Prince Cunobeline,[1] ruler
of the Trinobantes, before which the ancient
Britons, lacking specie of any kind, trafficked
with rings of iron[2] and plates of brass—*all* have
had their day, down to the sovereign of our own
times.

So have I given you, Reader, the coinage of
many minds, and if the black mail or copper
currency has not been *all* called in, I hope you
will at least find amongst it, one or two gold
farthings.

" EDWARD did smite round penny, halfpenny, farthing,
The Crosse passes the bond of all throughout the ring;
The king's side was his head, and his name in written,
The Crosse side what city it was in coyned and smitten.
To poor man, ne to priest, the penny frayeth nothing.
Men give God ay the least, they feast him with a farthing.
A thousand, two hundred, four score years and mo,
On this money, men wondered, when it first began to goe."

[1] This Prince Cunobeline lived, according to Stow, at
Camalodunum, now called Malden, in Essex, and flourished
about the time of Julius Cæsar, in imitation of whom, he
had his own image stamped upon this coin,—the first ever
made in England, and struck at Malden.

[2] Speed says that he himself had seen dug out of the earth,
in little cruses or pitchers, these rings and brass plates, the
substitutes for coin of the ancient Britons.

PRINTED BY WHITTINGHAM AND WILKINS,
TOOKS COURT, CHANCERY LANE.

www.ingramcontent.com/pod-product-compliance
Lightning Source LLC
Chambersburg PA
CBHW030400270326
41926CB00009B/1196